New Businesses Women Can Start and Successfully Operate

The Woman's Guide to Financial Independence

MARY LESLIE & DAVID D. SELTZ

H 487 **$3.95**
CANADA **$4.95**

NEW BUSINESSES
WOMEN
CAN START AND
SUCCESSFULLY OPERATE

the text of this book is printed
on 100% recycled paper

NEW BUSINESSES
WOMEN
CAN START AND
SUCCESSFULLY OPERATE

The Woman's Guide
to Financial Independence

by

Mary Leslie and David D. Seltz

BARNES & NOBLE BOOKS

A DIVISION OF HARPER & ROW, PUBLISHERS

New York, Hagerstown, San Francisco, London

HF5356
L46
1979x

First BARNES AND NOBLE BOOKS edition published 1979.

ISBN: 0-06-463487-6

79 80 81 82 83 10 9 8 7 6 6 5 4 3 2 1

TABLE OF CONTENTS

8. FOOD—FASCINATING, VITAL, PROFITABLE 123

9. WRITING—THE PEN IS MIGHTIER THAN THE SWORD—MORE PROFITABLE, TOO 141

10. OPPORTUNITIES FOR THE ORGANIZER 155

11. PUTTING YOUR OFFICE KNOW-HOW TO WORK 165

1.

WOMEN'S NEW ROLE

The third quarter of the Twentieth Century is an excellent time to be a woman. Everything in this dynamic period is happening faster and faster and that includes new opportunities for women. Practically *nothing* is barred to you now, if you are a woman.

Acceptance of women in politics, business, and the professions is accelerating. At the end of 1975, Worldwatch Institute reported that in 129 countries around the world women vote on equal terms with men. Compare this with 1960, when women had suffrage in only 92 countries, 69 countries in 1950, and 30 in 1940. 1974 was the year Ella T. Grasso was elected Governor of Connecticut, the first woman to be chosen for such office not as the widow or shadow of a distinguished man but strictly on her own. That same year Mary Anne Krupsak became Lieutenant-Governor of New York State. There are 17 women in the House of Representatives.

Women have been in the United States armed forces since World War II but only in 1975 were the first women

cadets accepted at West Point. More and more women are
going into law and women judges have been on the scene for
some years—United States District Judge Sarah T. Hughes
administered the Oath of Office to President Lyndon B.
Johnson in 1963—but in 1975 a woman was seriously considered as a nominee for the Supreme Court to succeed Justice
William Douglas. Early in 1976, Anne Armstrong was
confirmed as the first woman Ambassador to Great Britain.

Medicine . . . banking . . . insurance . . . police work . . .
the merchant marine . . . all are open now to women. Some
denominations are ordaining women ministers. Engineering is
supposedly still a predominantly masculine preserve, yet
Meredith M. Homet, business manager of *Women's Work*
magazine, is quoted in a recent interview: "We could employ
any female engineer who walked in the door, we get so many
requests for them."

UP THE CORPORATE LADDER

Management? *Business Week* is so impressed with the
women getting to the top here—for instance, Marion S.
Kellogg, vice-president of General Electric, and Diane D.
Levine, staff vice-president of Continental Airlines—that they
have instituted a regular department, The Corporate Woman,
dedicated to such high powered females, exploring in depth
how they—and their masculine colleagues—can best adjust to
this new allocation of authority. *Business Week* believes that
more and more women will make it up the corporate ladder,
even though at that time, out of 2,500 presidents, vice-presi-
dents, and chairpersons of major corporations, only 15 or so
were women. However, indications are that the United States
is ceasing to underutilize the talents of half its adult population, the magazine pointed out.

Women, at least some of them, are doing well at keeping
ahead of inflation. *New Woman* magazine has surveyed some
feminine annual incomes in 1974, including: Mary Keefe,
Commanding Officer, New York City Police Sex Crimes Unit,

$21,651; Billie Jean King, tennis pro, $175,225; Barbara Walters, formerly of TV's "Today" and "Not For Women Only," $400,000.

Women in occupations generally thought of as more feminine are also hitting the high brackets, such as Elaine Monroe, fashion buyer for Bloomingdale's, $30,000; Beverly Ann Johnson, model for publications like *Glamour, Vogue, Harper's Bazaar,* $100,000; Bette Midler, singer, appearing for Minskoff Theatres, half a million dollars for four weeks of her ten-week engagement.

So, you see, whether you are a Freiden-follower or a Total Woman, or alternate between the two extremes, opportunities, economic and otherwise, are not lacking in the current scene.

SOME GLOOM STILL PREVAILS

Of course, *all* the news is not good yet. According to a Conference Board report released in 1975, the earning gap between men and women—surprise—actually widened in the last two decades. Men's average yearly earnings: $11,800; women's: $6,800. That puts women (on the average) 43% below men, whereas twenty years ago women earned only 36% less than men.

Why should this be, in the face of all the brilliant individual success and all the legal reform there has been?

The Conference Board accounts for the increased discrepancy by the arrival of a new mix of working women. In the 1950's most working women were either well educated or worked out of a need to support themselves, whereas now there is a much broader base of women in the labor force, representing nearly all ages and levels of education. College-trained women account for only 42% of the growth in the female work force. Women with a high school education, or less, make up 58% of the increase, and most of them have taken relatively low-paying jobs.

So there you have it. There's still no royal road to financial success. Well, who expects anything but to work to attain a goal? ("Management style?" *Business Week* quotes Diane D. Levine, "If I have any style, it's to work my tail off.")

LIB MOVEMENT, EARLY AMERICAN STYLE

The fact is that some American women always have worked, and for money, too. In colonial and pioneer days, women who had to support themselves and others could teach, become seamstresses or milliners, open a store, enter domestic service, or keep a tavern or boarding house, not to mention taking up an older and less respectable trade. But these efforts did not promote standing in the best society and women were denied the vote.

In 1776, just prior to national independence, Abigail Adams bent her powdered head over her desk and wrote to her husband John concerning the plans for the new government: "If particular care and attention is not paid to the Ladies, we are determined to foment a Rebellion, and will not hold ourselves bound by any laws in which we have no voice or Representation."

This gave John a hearty laugh.

A POKE BONNET SPARKS A STRIKE

A century later, by 1876, men were still laughing at the idea of women outside the home, although the first Women's Rights Convention had been held at Seneca Falls, New York in 1848; bloomer girls had made a gesture toward dress reform, and Susan B. Anthony and others were at work on public opinion. As for jobs, in 1817, three power looms in Fall River, Massachusetts were operated by women; in 1834, in Lowell, Massachusetts, a girl tossed her poke bonnet out of a factory window, a signal that the other women were to leave their looms and go on strike. New Jersey early in its statehood, granted its women the vote, but the men had second thoughts and rescinded the privilege in 1807.

Late in the Nineteenth Century came the introduction of the typewriter, an invention that did as much, perhaps more, than the franchise to bring women out of the home and into earning power. The female typist, in her Gibson Girl shirt-waist, became an accepted part of the office.

HOW ABOUT BEING YOUR OWN BOSS?

In the current success stories, there is another category—the self-employed woman.

Corporate management, politics, the law courts, the stage, communications, all have their lure. But for some, true independence lies in being one's own boss. The financial returns of self-employment, while they may be sizable, probably will not match some of the salaries of outstanding employees. Still, the self-employed worker, man or woman, can choose full-time, part-time, or spare time occupations; can operate a business part-time for some years, say, while children are growing up, and then expand it to consume as much time as desired; can adjust hours and holidays to suit an individual schedule; select a business possible to operate from home and save rent and lease expense and stay snug in bad weather instead of battling the elements on the way to work.

No temperamental superior will harass the self-employed, although a fractious customer or client might. True, risks are very much present in self-employment, but so are possible gains, not only financially but in life style. This field has its share of women successes, like Lillian Vernon, who has nursed a mail order belt, bag and jewelry business, begun at home, into a major enterprise with a payroll of 160 and an average Christmas business of 75,000 packages. Evelyn Squire Culp administers her own business school on the lower floor of her spacious house in Westchester County. Every locality can produce like examples.

This book is for the woman who wants to work on her own. Most of the careers suggested might be adopted by either men or women, but since the subject is Woman, let's keep it that way.

KNOW THYSELF

What type of woman wants to be, and is suited to be self-employed?

This sort of self-expression might appeal to you if you are in the "Life must hold something better than a nine-to-five desk job" group.

Or perhaps you are gainfully employed but not as gainfully as the men on your level, and with no prospect of change in the near future.

Perhaps you have never worked—for money, that is—and are casting about to see if you have any skills that can be turned into cash.

You might be a housewife who wants to expand at least your financial horizon and are contemplating some form of marketable output.

Widows, divorcees, women wanting to supplement Social Security are others who may be seekers for fulfillment in the ranks of the self-employed.

That hyphenated word takes in a wide range of work. Try to analyze yourself.

Is glamour your scene, like work with high fashion, party planning and giving, or interior decoration?

Do you like the challenge and detective work of research —literary, social, or commercial?

Are you creative?

Are you fitted to take advantage of the present day boom in handicrafts?

Is food your fancy?

Are you a writer?

Are you a good organizer?

Do you want to put your office skills to work for yourself?

Can you sell?

Can you put over a promotion?

Do you enjoy working with the furry, feathered, and finny friends of petdom?

Can you teach people (big and little)?

Into which group would your personality and skills fall? There are many occupations that can be self-employed under each category. By generally classifying yourself, you will get an idea of work that you will enjoy. Self-employment is self-expression and there is no point in it unless you basically *like* the work. Your educational and financial background matters, too, of course. Some kinds of work require long and expensive training. Others need previous experience, while some need very little specific preparation.

Next, have you the kind of personality traits that any self-employment requires? The United States Small Business Administration, in their Rating Scale for Evaluating Personal Traits Important to the Proprietor of a Business, has worked out a list of pertinent questions which you should consider. (See page 15.)

The quiz master who formulated this rating scale should have added another query: "Can I be objective in regard to myself?'' which hardly anybody can, especially the enthusiastic, self-confident type wanting to go into business for herself (or himself). But do your best to size yourself up. Positive answers should heavily predominate, naturally, but don't be discouraged at a few downers. Even, to take an extreme example, if the "attitude toward others" response is as bad as possible—i.e., "inclined to be quarrelsome or uncooperative"—this *might* be linked to "highly creative." If so, you know right now that you need a sweet, understanding, patient, long-suffering partner to put up with you and make the actual contacts with the public in marketing your creations.

Rating Scale for Evaluating Personal Traits Important to the Proprietor of a Business

INSTRUCTIONS: Place a check mark on the line following each trait where you think it ought to be. The check mark need not be placed directly over one of the guide phrases, because the rating may lie somewhere between the phrases.

Initiative	Additional tasks sought; highly ingenious	Resourceful; alert to opportunities	Regular work performed without waiting for directions	Routine worker awaiting directions
Attitude toward others	Positive; friendly interest in people	Pleasant, polite	Sometimes difficult to work with	Inclined to be quarrelsome or uncooperative
Leadership	Forceful, inspiring confidence and loyalty	Order giver	Driver	Weak
Responsibility	Responsibility sought and welcomed	Accepted without protest	Unwilling to assume without protest	Avoided whenever possible
Organizing ability	Highly capable of perceiving and arranging fundamentals in logical order	Able organizer	Fairly capable of organizing	Poor organizer
Industry	Industrious: capable of working hard for long hours	Can work hard, but not for too long a period	Fairly industrious	Hard work avoided
Decision	Quick and accurate	Good and careful	Quick, but often unsound	Hesitant and fearful
Sincerity	Courageous, square-shooter	On the level	Fairly sincere	Inclined to lack sincerity
Perseverance	Highly steadfast in purpose; not discouraged by obstacles	Effort steadily maintained	Average determination and persistence	Little or no persistence
Physical energy	Highly energetic at all times	Energetic most of time	Fairly energetic	Below average

The Seltz Organization, Inc., of New York, has a similar questionnaire:

QUESTIONS TO ASK YOURSELF

	YES	NO
1. Can I manage my own business?		
a. Can I organize my time to get many things done?	( )	( )
b. Can I get down to handling the details that any business of my own requires?	( )	( )
c. Do I have the initiative and energy required?	( )	( )
2. Am I truly suited to the type of activity the business requires of me? For example:		
Selling people ideas	( )	( )
Selling people products	( )	( )
Offering services	( )	( )
Figure work	( )	( )
Work with hands	( )	( )
Supervising others	( )	( )
Inside my own house or place	( )	( )
Outside, moving around	( )	( )
Traveling	( )	( )
3. Am I financially equipped for the business I'd like?		
a. Do I have the cash needed to get started?	( )	( )
b. Can I pay financing charges without undue hardships?	( )	( )
c. Do I have enough operating capital?	( )	( )
d. Can I cover living expenses for the first year?	( )	( )
4. Am I entering a market that promises continued growth?	( )	( )

YES NO

5. Can I perform as well as (or better than) the
   others I may know in this business? ( ) ( )

6. Am I qualified to promote this business
   properly? ( ) ( )

7. Have I a good chance to meet local
   competition? ( ) ( )

8. Does my lawyer consider the business a proper
   venture? ( ) ( )

9. Can the business provide, or increase, a
   satisfactory standard of living for me, or my
   family (if I have one)? ( ) ( )

10. Will I and my family be reasonably content
    with the status or "image" of the type of
    business? ( ) ( )

11. Will my work hours allow me sufficient time
    with my family, or myself if I am single? ( ) ( )

12. Does my husband share my enthusiasm for the
    business? ( ) ( )

13. Is my accountant satisfied with the earnings
    prospect? ( ) ( )

14. This question to be answered only if the
    business is a husband-and-wife operation.
    If the answer is "no," this is not the business
    for you:

    Can I expect my husband's wholehearted
    help in the business? ( ) ( )

How to score yourself: Give yourself 6 points for each "yes." If your total score is less than 72, think twice before you go into business for yourself.

This quiz includes the important elements of finance and family relations. Both have to be considered. Finance can loom very large in some beginning businesses, like opening a boutique. If there is a man in the picture and/or children, a favorable emotional climate in regard to him or them is vital to your success. However, this situation is not as difficult as it used to be. Children are adjusting all the time to working mothers. Men are gladder and gladder to receive help in the increasingly precarious task of balancing the family budget. Inflation can do more to break down male chauvinism than a Women's Lib parade.

2.

NEED TO SHAKE THE MONEY TREE?

Sandra Smith wants to go into business. Her children are in school, which gives her more free time but means that college and its expenses are ahead, so she would like to add to the family earnings. Sandra plans to open a dress shop in her neighborhood, where she knows many people, their circumstances, and tastes, and she has noted that there is no shop selling dresses and accessories nearer than about a mile on foot and half an hour at least by bus, counting waits and traffic involvements. Sandra, before her marriage, was secretary to a buyer in women's wear, so she knows something of the wholesale market, seasonal buying, movement of stock and so on. She has a site in mind, on the street floor of a small office building with large display window space, in walking distance of nearby apartment and two-family houses, and with parking space at the back.

For this kind of business, Sandra needs capital, for down payment on a lease, for painting and carpeting the interior attractively, for dress racks, mirrors in the dressing room, and at least one showcase for accessories and costume jewelry.

TO BORROW OR NOT TO BORROW

Of course, the best way for Sandra to raise capital is to take it out of her own savings—if any. Since she would be borrowing from herself, there would be no interest and no time payments coming up at relentless intervals, and she need not put up security.

However, perhaps with family expenses and inflation Sandra and her husband have not been able to save any substantial sum. So she goes to the bank where she and her husband have a joint account, and explains her project to one of the bank's officials.

IF THE BANK SAYS "YES"

The banker applies what is called the "3 C's" to Sandra's case—Character, Capital, and Capacity to pay. The first of these involves her personal integrity and, since she and her husband have banked there for several years and the banker knows them in the community, he is confident of that intangible but vital asset. "Capital" takes in the collateral Sandra can offer, which might be the family dwelling if they own it, or their car, life insurance, or any stocks and bonds she owns.

"Capacity to pay" brings evaluation of her plan, the proposed location, and the background of experience Sandra would bring to it.

Sandra may obtain various types of loans from the bank: (1) short-term loan (payable in about 90 days); (2) long-term loan (extending for as long as ten years). Types of bank loans include:

1. *Straight Commercial Loans:* Based on submitting financial statement. This loan is generally used for seasonal financing or inventory expansion (usually 30 to 60 days).

2. *Installment Loans:* These are usually long-term loans, repaid on a monthly basis. These loans can be tailored to the business needs, for example, heavier repayments during peak months and smaller repayments during offseason periods.

3. *Term Loans:* Such loans have maturities of one to ten years and may either be secured or unsecured. Loan repayments may be made on almost any agreed-upon basis—monthly, quarterly, semi-annually, annually. Early repayments are often relatively small, with a large final payment. Although many term loans are backed by collateral security, the lender ordinarily requires that current assets exceed current liabilities in at least a 2-1 ratio.

4. *Bills Or Notes Receivable:* Promissory notes are often given for purchase of goods. These notes are called bills receivable or notes receivable. These can usually be discounted—that is, purchased by the bank. Your account is credited with the amount of the note less the discount to due date. The bank will collect from the note makers when it is due.

5. *Warehouse Receipt Loans:* Under this form of financing, goods are stored in warehouses and the warehouse receipt is given to the bank as security for a loan to pay off the supplier. As fast as the borrower is able to sell his merchandise he buys back portions of the inventory.

6. *Equipment Loans:* Loans are made to finance the purchase of machinery or equipment. The lender usually retains title until installment payments have been completed.

7. *Collateral Loans:* Based on such collateral as chattel mortgages on personal property, real estate mortgages,

life insurance (up to cash surrender value of the property) or stock and bonds.

IF THE BANK SAYS "NO"

But possibly Sandra and her husband are already in debt to the bank, having borrowed for the down payment on their house and later for their two cars. Although they are paying off these loans regularly, the banker points out that they still have some years to go and that they have already borrowed on their life insurance.

He feels that the bank cannot advance any more money, since the percentage of small businesses that fail is enough to make bankers cautious. He tells her, however, that there is another source of help. She can contact her local Small Business Administration Office. This is a government agency, geared to expedite loans (that are justifiable) for small businesses. They request, as the first step, that the applicant initiate the loan request at the local bank. If the bank says no, SBA will undertake, in many instances, to "share" the loan with the bank, assuming responsibility for 50% or more. The majority of banks (even those refusing an initial loan request) usually cooperate with SBA sponsored loans.

Another "prime" loan source is Small Business Investment Companies. SBIC's use partly private, partly federal money to provide capital for small businesses—through loans, direct stock purchases, or debentures convertible into stock. This gives you a loan-procurement opportunity formerly available only to bigger companies. These SBIC's are generally assisted by the Small Business Administration (authorized to buy up to $1,000,000 in debentures of an individual SBIC). Approximately 480 SBIC's are now in operation. Financing costs are generally higher than banks but often lower than other outside "private" sources. To obtain names and addresses of SBIC's in your area, write to the Small Business Administration, Investment Division, Washington, D.C. 20025, or to National Association of SBIC's, 537 Washington Building, Washington, D.C. 20005.

STILL OTHER LOAN SOURCES

Other means of obtaining loans for Sandra include:

1. *Private Capital:* She would insert an ad in her local newspaper under "Capital Wanted." Through this medium she can attract private investors who regularly consult this column for investment opportunities.

2. *Factors:* In each community there are factoring firms who make loans to all types of businesses. Their standards are lower than the banks', hence, they are more inclined to extend loans (even though the applicant may have been turned down by banks or government sources). Factors are recommended only as a last resort, since their interest rates are often excessive.

3. *Veterans Administration Loans:* Veterans of the armed forces may be eligible to obtain a loan via the local Veteran Administration Office. Write to them to obtain their detailed pamphlet on types of loans offered and controlling conditions.

4. *Insurance Companies:* Many insurance firms maintain loan departments as an important adjunct to their business. Their rates (although generally higher than banks') are much lower than those of factors and other loan sources.

5. *Commercial Investment Companies:* There are many investment companies, privately constituted, that grant loans. You will find them listed in your local telephone directories (Yellow Pages). Their rates are generally on a par with rates of factoring organizations.

6. *Leasing Firms:* "Leasing" has become more and more prominent in recent years. Almost any type of product or equipment can now be leased. Thus, it acts to:

Finance many aspects of your business—e.g., furniture, fixtures, machinery, equipment—giving you a period of three to five years to pay back via small monthly payments.

Finance your customers (particularly if the product cost is comparatively high). You (as the seller) are paid the full amount due, immediately. The customer pays the leasing company—over a period of years.

DO YOU REALLY NEED A LOAN?

Her banker advises Sandra, for the beginning of her project and for possible expansion later on: DON'T seek a loan unless the money is needed for specific business purposes that promise well. DO seek a loan if it helps establish the business, quickens progress, and expands profits. Bear in mind that it is good business to pay out "2X" dollars if "10X" dollars can be obtained in return.

Your own banker would give you the same advice. Sandra, planning a boutique, needs a fairly substantial loan. If her project were home-based—say, crafting handmade jewelry, writing free lance copy, or designing dresses or accessories—she would need a much lower sum, probably no loan at all.

ASK YOUR LAWYER!

Besides a banker, Sandra—and anyone else establishing a business—needs a lawyer, an accountant, and an insurance man (or woman).

In fact, she needs the lawyer before the banker, so as to be sure that not only the business but its location and operations conform to the laws of her state and municipality, such as zoning laws, fire, and health laws. Is a license required?

The lawyer will go into all this, advise whether or not the business should be incorporated, and explain the differences between a proprietorship, a partnership, and a corporation.

In general terms, a sole proprietor owns the business, is personally responsible for its functioning, and his or her personal property is subject to any law suit that might arise.

In a partnership, the business is shared between two or more partners. The disadvantage is that each partner is responsible not only for his or her own actions in connection with the business, but may be equally responsible for those of the other partner or partners, and personal property is still vulnerable in a law suit.

A corporation, on the other hand, makes the business a separate legal entity; a "person" apart from the person or persons who own and operate such corporation. Generally speaking, personal property is immune in any law suit, although, of course, corporation property is not. The cost of incorporating is relatively modest. It varies from state to state.

Different situations, personal or financial, call for different solutions of the problems of organizing a business. It is always wise, therefore, to have a lawyer's counsel and, in most cases, the advice of an accountant as well.

IS THIS POLICY NECESSARY?

To arrive at a decision as to how much insurance, and what type of insurance, is necessary for your business, consult a licensed representative of one of the leading insurance organizations. These representatives are trained to advise on the needs of individuals and the specific policies that best meet these needs. The kinds of insurance usually necessary are: fire insurance, liability insurance, automobile insurance, workman's compensation insurance, life insurance, health insurance, and pensions. If you conduct your business from home, discuss with your insurance advisor as to whether the insurance on your residence also covers the commercial venture you are undertaking, or if policy adjustments are necessary.

You need an accountant to help you at tax time and to advise you in the complexities of business finance, although you probably will do your own day-to-day bookkeeping. The Small Business Administration has issued what might be called an elementary course for double-entry bookkeeping, as follows:

Assets, Liabilities, and Capital: Anything a business *owns* that has a money value is an *asset* of the business. Cash, merchandise, supplies, amounts owed by customers (accounts receivable), land, buildings, furniture and fixtures, delivery equipment, and so on are assets.

Anything the business *owes* is a *liability*. Liabilities might include amounts owed to suppliers (accounts payable) or to the bank (notes payable), taxes already incurred but not yet due for payments, wages earned by employees since the last payday, and other amounts due.

The difference between what the business *owns* and what it *owes* is the amount that really belongs to the owner of the business—his *equity* or *capital*.

The Framework For Your Records: Liabilities can be thought of as creditors' rights or claims against the assets of the business, and capital as the owner's rights. The sum of these rights to the assets, of course, will always equal the sum of the assets themselves. In other words—

$$\text{Assets} = \text{Liabilities} + \text{Capital}$$

Suppose you pay a $50 bill from a supplier. One of your assets—cash—will be reduced by $50. But a liability—accounts payable—will be reduced by the same amounts, so the equation will still balance.

Now suppose you buy $50 worth of supplies and pay cash for them. Again, the asset cash will be reduced by $50; but in this case, the value of another asset—supplies—will be increased by $50. So the sum of all the assets doesn't change, and the equation still holds true.

This equation is known as the accounting equation.

The Basic Records: The financial records of a business begin with bits and pieces of paper—sales checks, credit memos, cash register tapes, written receipts, check stubs, petty cash slips, bank statements, and so on. These papers are important. Some sort of written record, however informal, should always be made *at the time a transaction takes place.*

The Journal: The information from these various papers is first brought together in one or more journals—sometimes called "books of original entry." A journal is simply a record of the daily transactions of the business. Each journal entry shows: (1) the date of the transaction, (2) a brief description of it, (3) the amount of money involved and, (4) the assets, liabilities, capital, or type of income or expense affected by the transaction.

The Ledger: To make the information recorded in the journal more usable, the entries are later transferred, or *posted* to a ledger account. Each *account* is a record of the increases and decreases in *one type* of asset, liability, capital, income, or expense. A book or file in which a number of accounts are kept together is called a *ledger.*

A business uses as many accounts as it needs for keeping track of its operations. A small firm with few pieces of equipment, for instance, may have only one account for all its equipment. A business with only one owner will need only one capital account; a partnership will need a capital account for each partner.

Double-Entry Bookkeeping: Notice that each of the transactions used to illustrate the accounting equation had two effects. This is true of all business transactions. Double-entry bookkeeping shows this twofold effect by recording every transaction twice—as a *debit* entry in one account and as a *credit* entry in another. Either or both of the entries may be broken down into several items, but the total of the amounts entered as debits must equal the total of the amounts entered as credits.

Debit and Credit Entries: One account may have both *debit* (*dr.*) and *credit* (*cr.*) entries. Then what determines whether an entry is to be a debit or a credit? It depends on the type of account and on whether the transaction to be entered will increase or decrease the account. The following table shows the types of entries (debit or credit) and the typical balances for each class of accounts:

Type of Account	If Transaction Will Decrease Account, Enter It As A:	If Transaction Will Increase Account, Enter It As A:	Typical Balance
Asset	Credit	Debit	Debit
Liability	Debit	Credit	Credit
Capital	Debit	Credit	Credit
Income	Debit	Credit	Credit
Expense	Credit	Debit	Debit

Thus, when you pay a bill, the amount is entered as a *debit* to accounts payable and as a *credit* to cash. When you buy supplies for cash, the amount paid is entered as a *debit* to supplies and as a *credit* to cash.

Each account sheet in the ledger has two columns for dollar amounts. *Debit* entries are always put in the left-hand dollar column and *credit* entries in the right-hand column. If the debit entries in an account total more than the credit entries, the account is said to have a *debit balance*. If the credit entries total more than the debit entries, the account has a *credit balance*. The total of all the credit balances must equal the total of all the debit balances.

The Trial Balance: To make certain that the sum of the debit balances does equal the sum of the credit balances, a trial balance is taken at the end of the month (or other accounting period). This is done by adding all debit account balances and all credit account balances. If no errors have been made, the two totals will be the same.

Financial Statements: The journal gives you a quick record of all your business transactions in order. The ledger accounts group the transactions of your business in such a way that at any time you can prepare a *balance sheet* and a *profit and loss statement*.

The balance sheet summarizes your assets, liabilities, and capital to show the condition of your business on a given date —how much of the assets you really own. It is called a balance sheet because it shows how the two sides of the accounting equation (assets = liabilities + capital) balance in your business.

The profit and loss statement summarizes the income and expenses of the business during a given period and the profit or loss that resulted.

By comparing your financial statements for this year with those for last year or with the financial statements of similar businesses, you can tell whether your business is getting better or worse and where it needs improvement.

THE ACCOUNTANT IS THE DOCTOR

Taxes, of course, are always with us and always changing. Therefore, you need the regular services of a professional accountant to guide you in this maze.

Some business people think of accountants as merely doing the taxes and overseeing the bookkeeping. Your accountant can help more than this, by bringing into the picture his perspective of business operations. A sort of doctor-patient relationship can develop. A business, like a person, can be sick without realizing it. The accountant is the doctor and, to continue the analogy, the sooner the condition is detected, the greater the chance of cure. Also, the accountant's advice is sometimes crucial when it comes to consideration of whether to borrow from the bank for expansion or help in a bind.

If your business is unincorporated, your accountant will probably bring to your attention the Self-Employed Retirement Plan instituted by the government to help those who cannot look forward to a pension, as can employees of large companies. Any self-employed individual and/or operator of an unincorporated business or partnership is eligible, whether or not the business has employees. The passage of the Employee Retirement Income Security Act of 1974 allows self-employed individuals to make tax-free contributions to retirement funds of 15% of their earned income up to a maximum of $7,500 each year. Lower income self-employed individuals can put aside 100% of their earned income up to $750 per year. All the money you contribute is tax deductible and all the interest and/or dividends your contributions earn are exempt from taxes until you retire, when it is more than likely you will be in a lower tax bracket. Distribution will be made not earlier than age 59½ nor later than age 70½ (even if you have not actually retired). Each participant may name a beneficiary who will receive payment in the event of the participant's death. If no beneficiary has been named, the account becomes part of the estate of the deceased.

3.

IMAGE-MAKING

Definitions of the word "image" in The American Heritage Dictionary include, "The concept of someone or something that is held by the public," and, "The character projected by someone or something to the public." These are the meanings that Madison Avenue has given to "image," one of the most important words in the vocabulary of advertising and promotion.

Every person, every business, and every institution has an "image"—good or poor, vivid or dim—and success depends to a great extent on such an impression. Vast sums are spent in projecting, improving, or maintaining images, and some of the nation's best think power goes into highly sophisticated research in this direction.

A small business needs a good image as much as A.T.& T. or General Motors. And it all comes down to Have Something The Public Wants; Let The Public Know You Have It; See That The Public Can Obtain It Conveniently; and Deal With The Public In A Pleasant And Courteous Manner.

Simple? Hardly. If it was simple, all those consultant firms, advertising agencies, and public relations associates wouldn't be beating their brains out.

MARKETING: THE TOTAL CONCEPT

We go on to another Madison Avenue key word: Marketing. What is marketing? Marketing may be defined as a total concept of all means to promote a business, including advertising (on and off premises), public relations, direct mail, special projects, and relations with community, patrons, and employees. No one, say the Madison Avenue sages, uses his full marketing potential. But you can try.

Begin with what the Avenue calls Research and Analysis. Research hunts out the pertinent facts (such as, How many people could your business reach and what is their income status?), and Analysis is interpreting the facts (like, Can this type of citizen be educated to buy your product or service?).

Big business makes surveys and sends out questionnaires and samples, but for a small, beginning business, rule of thumb can serve. You know your locality, its income brackets, tastes, and transportation. Thus, an educated guess should not be too difficult. If you fear you are too starry-eyed, advice is available from those less so, to wit, your banker, your Chamber of Commerce, or the nearest headquarters of the Government's Small Business Association.

THE PROBLEM OF LOCATION

Next comes the problem of location, if you have not already considered it. This is a vital point. A poor, inaccessible location has killed many a business. A few pertinent points are: Is yours a business that will draw people to its location so that it does not depend too much on location? Is it a business that should be located among related businesses, even if they are remotely related, like the stores in a shopping center?

Remember that the expense of a location should be measured in terms of the ratio of rental to sales, rather than in terms of dollars cost per month. A low-rent location may prove very costly if customers are scarce; a high-rent location may prove inexpensive if the flow of customers keeps the cash register ringing.

Below are a few examples from a Table of Rent Averages, based on gross volume of sales:

TYPE OF BUSINESS	PERCENT
Apparel, children's or infants	5.00
Apparel, women's specialty	4.90
Beauty shops	6.45
Confectionery stores	2.91
Dairies	.55
Florists	2.50
Food Stores, specialty	4.00
Liquor stores	3.10
Furniture stores	5.10
Music stores	3.50
Gifts and novelty shops	6.20
Nursery and garden supplies	1.65
Jewelry stores	3.85
Paint, glass, and wallpaper stores	3.70
Photographic studio and supply shops	4.15
Restaurants	4.20
Shoe stores	4.75
Upholsterers	2.45
Variety stores	5.30

In assessing the purchasing power of the area, find out as much as you can about the volume of retail trade in the district; the number of telephone subscribers; number, age, and make of cars owned; number of bank depositors and volume of deposits; census reports of rents; school and utility figures.

Be sure to investigate tax and insurance rates. An otherwise attractive site might be impossible because of excessive taxes, community fees, and insurance rates. Call in your lawyer for professional advice on these matters.

How are the transportation and parking facilities?

A few more suggestions are: Have a talk with the local mail carrier, who is usually a good source of information; talk to other business people in the vicinity, including competitors; in general, avoid "dead spots," where shoppers don't pause to buy, like vacant lots, coal companies, parks, and strictly residential areas, churches, libraries, and public utilities offices.

Of course, if you have decided at least to *start* your business from home, your problem of seeking a location is solved, and your rent expenses cut out of your budget.

DRAW THE CUSTOMER'S EYE

Whether at home or elsewhere, no matter what the type of business, you must strive to make its headquarters attractive, both outside and inside, to avoid clutter, to use space efficiently, and not only to please but to challenge and interest a customer.

One important element is color. No matter how small your space, you can make it more effective by utilizing color for maximum value. Color creates emotional response. An extreme example is the case of a midwestern hospital which puts depressed patients in red rooms to cheer them up, excitable patients in rooms decorated in soothing blue.

Here are some findings on the effects of colors:

Red   — activity, warmth
Blue   — serenity, coolness

Purple — richness, dignity (royalty apparently knew this
centuries before the psychologists caught on)
Green — nature
Yellow — sunshine
Pink — health

Let us say that if you have red curtains, you change them
in the summer, perhaps to cool blue. If you have a natural
foods shop, you decorate in green for nature and yellow for
sunshine. One restaurant pleased its patrons by painting its
walls a cheery yellow and installing warm lighting, a combination flattering to the complexion and one that encourages
diners to relax and linger. A gift shop in a narrow store
painted the long walls in light blue, the narrow end wall a
warm brown, making the shop seem wider and banishing the
customers' feeling of claustrophobia.

After the decoration is decided on and installed, take a
fresh "customer's" look at your place of business. This is a
good thing to do periodically, as long as you stay there. How
does it look to the passer-by? Can you see need for improvement, simplification, spotlighting certain features?

Do you have proper signs, both interior and exterior?
Signs must tell and sell, be attractive and, above all, suited for
instant reading.

Do your windows say, "Come In! Come In!" Is there a
focal point to catch attention? Your windows are your own
free advertising and you need to get their full power of selling.

ADVERTISING—WHERE? HOW MUCH?

Other kinds of advertising are necessary, too, or at least
advisable. If, for any reason, you find yourself in an unfavor-
able location, advertising is a must and can do much to offset
the site's disadvantages and bring people to you. In fact,
advertising is a must, in any event.

When the owner of a small business advertises, he is probably only too aware that he is competing with million dollar accounts paying $70,000 for a minute of prime network television. The small business person has a modest budget, doesn't have an advertising department, and seldom uses an agency, usually prepares the ads, perhaps using mats and other aids provided by suppliers. This can be discouraging, and sometimes a negative attitude develops, the conviction that advertising costs too much and that you can never be sure of results.

This kind of thinking disregards a vital point of economics—the fact that advertising is the least expensive method of building sales volume, considered at cost per sale.

All right, then, how to go about it? The Bank of America's *Small Business Reporter's* pamphlet, "Advertising"* (which incidentally, will repay your detailed reading), advocates a step-by-step advertising plan:

Budgeting of your advertising expenses
Distribution of such funds
Preparation of ads
Choosing media
Assessing results

A recent survey published in this pamphlet shows respondents spending an average 3.1 percent of gross sales on advertising: retailers, 2.5 percent; service businesses, 3.5 percent. Businesses with gross sales under $25,000 spend 2.8 percent; $25,000 to $99,000, 3.8 percent; $100,000 to $259,000, 2.9 percent; over $250,000, 2.4 percent.

The newer the business, the more advertising it needs.

As for distribution, advertising funds should be allocated (1) to the month of the year, and (2) to the suitable media.

---

*"Advertising," *Small Business Reporter*, Bank of America, 1969.

Advertising expenditures should coincide with periods of high and low sales volume, higher during the part of the year when sales will probably be good. Advertising dollars have been wasted taking ads in off-season. Other times of high advertising might be in consideration of local events, i.e., centennials, fairs, theatre seasons, etc.

Write Your Own Copy?

Many small business people prepare their own ads. If you are going to do this, you need time, imagination, and use of free advertising aids from your suppliers.

First, who are you talking to? Do you want to reach homemakers, working people, dog owners, gardeners, gourmets, music lovers? In writing copy, try to persuade the readers as if you were talking to them directly.

Some important points in ad writing are:

- Challenging attention
- Telling why product or service is necessary—and attractive
- The call to buy NOW

Besides advertising merchandise, a business should advertise *itself*, its special individuality, such as quality, convenience, low price, prompt service. Always, the unique personality of the business itself should be emphasized. Communication devices for keeping the business image before the public, according to Bank of America's *Small Business Reporter,* include:

1. Slogans, some phrase immediately associated with the business
2. Logo or trademark, identified with the business
3. Radio jingle or tune, identified with the business
4. Individual artwork or layout
5. Television or radio dialogue in a unique style, like humor "kidding" the business

If becoming your own ad executive does not appeal, media space-and-time salespeople, skilled in ad techniques, will usually work with their clients. There are also small advertising agencies who specialize in the more modest accounts and will devote a generous amount of time to helping plan advertising campaigns.

Media, Media Everywhere

Since the major cost of advertising is the cost of media (media purchases make up about 90% of total advertising expenditure), you must select media with great care.

What you should try to do is to pinpoint your market.

What you don't want to do is pay for a circulation that goes beyond your market area (waste circulation) or reaches the wrong type of people for your product.

Good advertising, in whatever media, calls for consistency, frequent appearance, and coverage of the market area you wish to reach.

The usual media available to small business include: newspapers, direct mail, radio, television, yellow pages, magazines, and signs, outdoor and transit. Of course, such media are divided and subdivided to give many, many means of communication. Under newspapers, for instance, besides the familiar columns, you can consider shoppers, weeklies, Sunday supplements, religious and other nonprofit, school, and neighborhood publications. Outdoor advertising includes billboards and posters, store signs and the name of the business painted on trucks, banners, balloons, etc.

Before advertising in a specific publication or other medium, the small business person should obtain detailed figures on costs and coverage, and find out as much as possible about the results other advertisers have achieved.

Number One Medium—Newspapers!

Newspapers are the number one medium for small business, according to the *Reporter* survey. Eighty-two percent of respondents use one or more newspaper media and 31 percent two or more. In answer to the question, "Which media brought you the best results?," the majority said "newspapers."

Why?

Newspapers give the news and people are used to reading them.

Newspapers usually cover the small business person's market area, with little waste circulation.

Cost of advertising in newspapers is relatively low.

Newspapers are current and bring quick action from ads; can be carried around; purchased at a number of places; are an effective visual medium.

Disadvantages of newspapers as advertising media include: Ads must compete with others on the same page; you cannot be sure of your position on the page (unless you pay extra); circulation might be larger than the trading scope of your business, resulting in waste; duration of effectiveness is short, compared with, say, magazines.

Another Favorite—Yellow Pages

Respondents of the *Reporter* gave second place to the Yellow Pages as an advertising medium, many spending over half their ad budgets there. Every business with a telephone gets a free one-line listing in the classified section. Additional space must be paid for. Rates for telephone directory display advertising are based on the number of names the directory carries.

Radio, the Intimate Medium

Some advertisers find radio a successful means for selling their goods, others don't. Essential to successful use of radio is frequency of use. Among the advantages of radio are:

While a radio commercial is on the air it has no immediate competition.

Most people have a radio and radios are heard almost everywhere—not only at home but in the car, at the beach, or ballgame.

Radio is an intimate medium and is good for associating a slogan or tune with your business; radio is flexible, with opportunity to change copy and scheduling at short notice; radio may reach people who do not read the newspapers; like newspapers, radio's cost is relatively low.

Its major disadvantage is that the advertising is so short-lived.

Note: Radio stations' personnel will help you write your advertising script or will prepare taped commercials for a fee. Some announcers will talk off the cuff from fact sheets supplied by the advertiser.

Television—Its Glamour Beckons

Television, according to the *Reporter* survey, is the medium the majority of small businesses have not used but would like to try. Local networks are doing their best to make it easy for the small business ad to get into television by cooperating in and/or supervising commercials, and by offering joint sponsorship with other local businesses.

Magazines and Signs

Small business does not advertise in national magazines

as a rule, since their rates are too high and their circulation extends beyond the territory of many small businesses. However, there are neighborhood, school, fraternal, church or temple, and regional magazines whose rates are not excessive and which make good media for the advertising messages of many products and services.

As for signs, every business uses a sign at least once, to identify the business. There are also transit signs on buses and the outdoor billboard type. Their value depends a good deal on the type of business. Motels, for instance, rely heavily on road signs, and bakeries, schools, books, and other general advertising appears in buses.

Direct Mail—Varied, Personalized, Effective

Then there is direct mail, a major form of advertising and one that has many advantages. Its principal drawback is it does not promote the community goodwill that advertising in any of the other media generates. Publishers always have a soft spot for their advertisers, and many a mention in the news columns or even a feature story, if one is justified, comes to the faithful newspaper advertiser. Owners of local radio and television stations also can "service" their advertisers in various ways.

However, direct mail is a deservedly popular way of advertising. It is unshared and the prospective customer received your message with a minimum of distraction. Contents of the mailing piece can be arranged so the customer is led into the message and reads first things first. The mailing piece can be planned to allow enough space to tell your complete story, with pictures.

Direct mail advertising can be a booklet, circular, leaflet, postcard, blotter, reprint, order blank, or stuffer. It can take dozens of forms, all up and down the expense scale.

A good mailing list is essential to an effective direct mail campaign. A very fine one can be made from your own charge customers, coupon users, people requesting information, and other present and prospective customers. You can also make up lists from telephone and trade directories; notices in the daily press of weddings, births, social events; membership lists of business and social organizations; auto registrations, voters, and taxpayers. Demographic lists can be purchased or rented from list brokers.

Another source is BankAmericard. Merchant members of the program may make use of the customer list for their market area. Production of the mailer (it must be approved by BankAmericard) and postage are taken care of by the advertiser, addressing and mailing are done at Bank-Americard centers with these costs passed on to the merchant in subsequent billing.

As time goes on, you will probably develop your own mailing lists, adapted, culled, and added to in the way that best suits your individual business. A good mailing list is "good" only if it reaches the people you and your business need to reach. It is a waste of postage to contact people who may be too far away or are just not the type of customer to whom your offering would appeal.

As for layouts and design, there are printers who specialize in direct mail. Besides actually producing the piece, they can design it and even write the copy, if you wish, offer you a mailing list, and handle the mailing out. Costs vary with the different printers.

Word of Mouth, the Unsurpassed

There seems to be general agreement, according to the *Reporter*, that, no matter how brilliant media advertising may be, "word of mouth" advertising from happy customers is the most effective of all forms of advertising.

Importance of You

A famous consultant has compiled a list of ways to make people want to do business with you. They include:

Be a joiner. Identify yourself with the business and philanthropic organizations in your community. You'll enjoy meeting people and at the same time establish yourself as a pleasant, cooperative personality. And remember the names and faces of people you encounter. If this is difficult, buy one of the memory system books.

Give service, those little extra attentions that make a customer feel special. A follow-up note, a word of congratulation or condolence, a friendly phone call, all help.

Let people know that you keep your word. Live up to promises made.

Be consistent. Don't quote one customer one price and another customer a different one. The wind carries word of these things—and the result is not helpful.

Watch for new ideas and developments in your field and think how they can be adapted to interest special customers.

Be logical. The appeal of a cute, feminine approach wears thin very quickly in business.

Be punctual. If you have an appointment, get there on time.

Don't lecture. Whatever you are selling, don't deliver the pitch as a monologue. Make it a conversational exchange. You'll learn something about the customer's personality, likes, dislikes, and needs—without boring him or her.

Take notes. Keep an informal record of your clients in a

card file and check it over frequently. If a client hasn't bought for a long time, why not? It might be financial reverses, personal troubles, or even interest in a competitor. Each cause would call for a different approach.

Be a graceful loser. If you don't get a sale, be just as cordial as if you had been successful.

Capitalize on your "goldmine," that is, your present customers. They can give you referrals to friends and associates; keep on buying from you; become a friendly voice in the community, putting in many a good word for you and your business.

PUBLIC RELATIONS BEGINS AT HOME

The working woman, with happy and expanding community relations, just might be a little less happy in her home life. Most career women—a great many, anyway—do marry and confront the absentee wife problem. How to have a good life, both at home and abroad?

Of recent years, since both members of more and more couples are working outside the home, the operation of the house has been solved by the husband sharing the housework in a way that, even twenty years ago, he would have scorned. Among current newlyweds this attitude is becoming even more revolutionary, as shown in a quotation in an interview by the Associated Press of one pair, both of whom had just graduated from college. "We decided we'd go job hunting. Whoever found the best pay for the fewest hours would take it, and the other would be the housewife." Or possibly, the househusband.

So a new word enters the current vocabulary. If the husband is the one to stay home, and he assumes the running of the household, he earns the title of househusband.

There could be a number of reasons for a man becoming a househusband. One such man is taking his sabbatical year. His wife continues to work, so he shops, cooks, and cleans—for the specified period only, he asserts firmly. This househusband doesn't like the role.

Another reason could be the one given by the young couple interviewed by the Associated Press: if the girl got the better job. This man had not tried housekeeping at the time of the interview, so it is not known how he would adjust.

The reason most dangerous to an equable relationship would be if the husband is "resting" in the theatrical sense—in other words, is unemployed—while the wife continues to work. He may offer to keep house—to be strictly fair, he should make the offer—but, in this case, perhaps, the working wife should not accept such offer, at least in its entirety. While he is looking for a new job, a bruised ego and a consciousness of doing a lot of unpaid work will not help him.

And, speaking of unpaid work, in McCall's Magazine's *Moneytalks*＊ the question is raised, "How much is a housewife worth?" In dollars and cents, that is. It is pointed out that a wife who devotes years to cooking, cleaning, and taking care of children is not entitled to Social Security, under present laws; this despite the fact that the economists of the Chase Manhattan Bank broke down the jobs of a housewife into twelve separate tasks and, in 1966, estimated she was worth $8,285.68 a year, a figure which inflation raised to $13,391.56 at a later date. The National Organization of Working Women is trying to correct the situation, one of the beliefs being that if only one partner works outside the home, half the income should by law belong to the other partner. Representative Bella Abzug of New York introduced a bill urging Social Security for housewives.

In all fairness, if these laws are passed, should they not apply equally to the househusband?

＊"Moneytalks," *McCall's Magazine*, May, 1974.

Mike McGrady of New Rochelle, New York, recently became a househusband of his own free will. A newspaper columnist earning $35,000 a year, he had (and still has) a working wife, Corinne. Corinne's enterprise is designing, making, and marketing plastic objects such as magazine racks, tables, picture frames, and see-through cookbook holders. When her business became sufficiently prosperous, Mike decided to try letting her be sole breadwinner, while he took over the house.

The day after he left the paper, his name appeared in a news story and he was referred to as "former columnist Mike McGrady." The words, he says, had a strange impact. He was a "former something" because he was a "current nothing, a suburban househusband."

Mike, however, stuck to his purpose and has written a book on his new life, "The Kitchen Sink Papers."* The *New York Times* reviewer, searching this lighthearted book for social significance, is impressed by finding that "the McGradys never questioned the generally agreed upon conceit that 'breadwinner' is more important than 'homemaker.' " In other words, the breadwinner, male or female, is the dominant partner.

Househusband?

In line with chairperson, Congressperson, businessperson, should there not be a unisex word instead of housewife or househusband?

Housespouse!

---

*"The Kitchen Sink Papers," Doubleday & Co., 1975.

A PLAN FOR SETTING UP YOUR OWN BUSINESS

The following pages describe various businesses that have a favorable earning potential and in most cases require minimal capital investment. They are diversified in subject and are intended to offer opportunity to a wide range of talents and time, whether the business is operated from home, in spare time, or from a more elaborate business structure, full time.

In determining earnings potential of each of these businesses, bear in mind the following:

1. Establish your START-UP COSTS, inclusive of:

   - Rent security (often 3 to 5 months in advance)
   - Fixtures and equipment
   - Starting inventory
   - Office supplies
   - Decorating and remodeling
   - Deposits for utilities
   - Legal and professional fees
   - License and permits
   - Advertising for the opening
   - Operating cash
   - Owner's withdraw during pre-start-up time

2. Next, establish your operating expenses for that particular business. In operating expenses it is advisable to include:

   a. Fixed expenses:
      - Rent (including rent security)
      - Utilities
      - Salaries (if any)
      - Vehicle rental or purchase cost (or operating cost if you already have your own car)
      - Insurance
      - Supplies

b. Next, establish your variable expenses, inclusive of:
- Operating supplies
- Gross wages
- Repairs and maintenance
- Advertising
- Car and delivery
- Bad debts
- Administrative and legal
- Outside labor
- Miscellaneous expenses

The Small Business Administration, that ever-present helper, has issued Small Marketers Aid No. 71, which includes a formalized check list for those going into business, with starting costs which you only pay once, as well as estimated monthly expenses.

Now that you have established operating expenses, determine potential income. The difference between this estimated income and the operating expenses will help establish whether or not the business can earn a satisfactory net profit. Keep in mind that you should know your Operating Ratios. These provide percentages indicating average expenditures by similar businesses (based on different levels of gross sales) and constitute guidelines to refer to in establishing your own levels of expenditure. A list of current operating ratios is available from Dun and Bradstreet, also from National Cash Register.

If you are planning to go into business, it is important to establish profit potential. The following profit margins are frequently applicable:

- If you are selling products—profit margin varies from 33% to 50%.

- If you are selling services—profit margin can vary from 50% to 200%.

● Your break even point is that point wherein you have covered all your expenses, and everything earned from that point on is considered profit.

Small Business Administration advises those considering going into business to draw up a Business Plan. The conception and formation of such a Plan, SBA maintains, provides a pathway to profit. The prospective owner-manager asks herself such questions as: Just what is my business—what service do I provide? Where is my market? Who will buy? Who is my competition? What is my sales strategy? What merchandising methods will I use? How much money is needed to operate my firm? How will I get the work done? And many more.

It takes time and patience to work out such a Plan, but there are compensating advantages: (1) The Plan gives you a path to follow; (2) makes it easy to explain your project to your banker through his or her reading or hearing the details of your Plan; (3) can help you communicate your aims and goals to employees, suppliers, and others; and, above all, (4) develops your ability to make judgments and stimulates constructive thinking about competitive conditions, promotional opportunities, and other pertinent matters. This pamphlet on the Business Plan is SBA's Small Marketer's Aid No. 153 and might very well be in your kit of literature for both starting and continuing a business.

4.

FROM THE GLAMOUR POINT OF VIEW

ART GALLERY

The Idea:

Has your community a painters' club, a group of enthusiasts who express themselves in portrait, landscape, and abstract art? If so, they no doubt have annual exhibits where paintings are displayed and hopes run high for sales.

Too often these hopes are dashed because the pictures were only shown a week or so and because the number of paintings that can be displayed in this yearly show is limited.

How about giving these painters a better chance and making some money for yourself at the same time? If you open a gallery where pictures are on display all year 'round, with promotion and advertising, you can look to receive a steady flow of paintings, which you will offer for sale on commission. There is a good chance you might prosper. People are buying more original paintings than in the past, especially if they are moderately priced.

Getting Started:

First, survey your source of suppliers, i.e., local artists. If you don't already know them, you can contact them through their club and art schools, museums, and stores selling art materials.

Then you need the gallery. If you don't find suitable space priced low enough, try asking a furniture store or a hotel or motel to *give* you wall space in return for the publicity they will receive. This publicity could be substantial if you can write good news releases. In any case, encourage reporters to visit your exhibitions. Interest them in writing stories and taking photographs of the pictures and of successful artists. Play up your grand opening and subsequent exhibits of special interest.

Advertise as much as you can afford. Use direct mail a lot, your mailing lists comprising names from the society columns, doctors, lawyers, teachers, the clergy, everyone in the higher cultural and/or income brackets. Send out announcements several times a year, whenever you have new paintings you think will intrigue them.

You should have at least two hundred paintings on display at all times. If you hang them without framing, this removes one headache. Make a deal with a framing establishment and send your customers on to them.

The Cash Flow:

Paintings are usually sold on a commission basis, with the seller receiving 40%. Your lawyer will draw up a routine written commission agreement, to be signed by all your painter clients.

If you price your paintings $25 to $250, none higher, you will probably do better than if you try for bigger prices. It is more important to keep the paintings moving.

PARTY PLANNING

The Idea:

Have you a knack for throwing original parties? If you have, you can put the talent to work for you. Probably you are frequently asked by friends to help with their parties and by local organizations when they want to put on a big bash. If you decide to go pro, you can have a lot of fun and get paid for it.

Getting Started:

Of course, you must come up with colorful and individual ideas. How about designing your parties around a "theme?" Like a newspaper party, with the invitations, menus, decorations all made from newspaper pages or cut out type, and games planned around news events? Or, for a birthday party, feature an amusing biography of the celebrant printed on one of those mock newspaper pages with big headlines. For a Merrie Olde England party, the invitations could be on scrolls, the refreshments include Nut Brown Ale and English foods, Elizabethan decorations, and so on. Costume parties of periods from the Stone Age to the 1920's, from pirates to hillbillies—the possibilities are endless. Or, you might stress wish fulfillment, such as Come as the Person You Would Like To Be, or Would Hate To Be.

Besides the theme parties, there are enough "plain" parties to be organized—a bridge tournament, a ball for some fraternal organization, an awards dinner. All these take administrative talent to make them go smoothly, working with caterers, orchestras, entertainers, decorations. Have the chairs delivered from the chair rental firm.

The best promotion is word of mouth, with newspaper advertising a close second. Finally, when you are established, you might consider assembling a catalog of completely "packaged" parties and try for a mail order business.

The Cash Flow:

Your expenses, besides advertising and the cost of the catalog, if you issue one, include party packages comprising imprinted invitations, place mats, decorations, and printed instructions for entertainment.

Fees can begin at $50 for a very simple party and go to $1,000 and up for bigger affairs. An especially planned party calls for a higher fee, of course.

AMUSEMENT DIRECTORY

The Idea:

If you have access to a mimeograph or Xerox machine, you can do what perhaps you have always wanted to do: design and lay out a little magazine. The upper row of the typewriter keys will give you ideas for decoration of the cover and at the top of each page. Purchase, or cut, typewriter paper the size you want for your magazine. When you type in the material, allow plenty of white space to show your art work effectively and make the page easy to read—and you're ready for the content of the magazine.

What shall it be? How about an Amusement Directory? This can be fun and profitable, too.

Getting Started:

If you live in a major city like New York or Chicago, better stick to listing the amusements of your neighborhood, but if you live in a small city or town, then take them all in— movies, cocktail lounges, restaurants with entertainment, concerts, dances, bowling alleys, public tennis courts, whatever is offered. Contact owners of local radio and television stations, explain your project and get them to send you their announcements regularly. Break the items down into departments, like movies, night spots, sports, and so on, and display each attractively on your pages.

The Cash Flow:

How do you make money? Sell advertising to the entertainment places, assuring them of wide circulation by distributing copies, free, to motels, hotels, airports, bus stations, dining spots, and community centers. Aim for 24 pages, including eight pages of ads. Calculate your expenses, which are low, perhaps just the paper and stencils and the charge for mimeograph or Xerox service. If you deliver the copies to the various centers yourself, you do not need postage or delivery service. Your charge for advertising might be $10 to $15 per inch, $50 to $75 for a half-page, $90 to $125 for a full page.

Besides the advertising revenue, you'll probably get free tickets to the various events and this may inspire you to write reviews and advance notices and thus extend the space and interest of your publication.

PLANNING AND ARRANGING WEDDINGS

The Idea:

If ever a pageant should go smoothly, it is the formal wedding, with its glamor and traditions, the bride in white satin and veil, the bridesmaids lovely in colors, the altar decked with flowers and aglow with candles, the solemn giving of the ring, and the heart-lifting procession down the aisle afterward. If all goes well, here is a beautiful and moving spectacle that will linger forever in the memory of those attending. Unfortunately, any hitch can mar or even spoil the occasion. To plan a formal wedding adequately may be a demanding and exhausting task that develops into a nightmare for the bride's mother, or whoever is in charge.

Here is a chance for a woman who has a turn for organization and a love of beauty and tradition to offer a service that can interest, even fascinate her and bring relief to the harried.

Getting Started:

If planning and arranging beautiful weddings seems your

field, the first thing to do is to summon up your memories of other weddings, your own, perhaps, and those of your friends and kin. Consult the etiquette books in the public library.

Call to mind and systematize all the intricacies of preparation, beforehand and on the actual wedding day. You need to consider invitations, decorations for church and reception, catering, flowers, music, photography, publicity, transportation. If you are to be an efficient supervisor, you must know just the right people—florists, photographers, limousine service—to call on. This means seeking out and arranging terms with all those businesses. By this time you can see that you would like to have, if possible, three to six months to work on a big wedding, although it could be done, under pressure, in three or even two weeks.

When you ponder all the details of the wedding day, with the bride and bridesmaids dressing at the bride's home, the preparations and decorating of the church, getting ready for the reception, you realize that you can't be in all those places at once. You need some associates. A successful wedding planning enterprise claims the services of three women, who work together, each handling separate phases of the preparation and actual occasion.

A schedule for the rehearsal and wedding should be mimeographed and given out to the wedding party and all concerned, such as photographers and transportation people. An example:

Rehearsal: 8 p.m., Monday (or whatever evening precedes the wedding date) at Such and Such church.

Wedding Day: 11:30 a.m. A supervisor arrives at church with checks for organist and sexton. Boutonniers for groom and ushers have been delivered with the altar flowers. Groom and ushers arrive at church.

12:30—bride and bridesmaids arrive at church.

1 p.m.—Bridal procession. After ceremony, wedding party comes down aisle, stands in room off vestibule until guests have left. Bride, groom, and party return to altar for photographs, then proceed in limousines to reception. Supervisor pays drivers.

Reception:

2 p.m.—receiving line forms: bride's mother, groom, maid of honor, best man. Bar is open.

2:45—bridal tables seated and buffet open for guests.

3:30—champagne served and cake cut by bride and groom and served.

There should be a guest book at the reception, which goes to the bride's family.

Dozens of other details will arise, of course, to be dealt with as they come. A challenge, but bringing off a lovely wedding can be a rewarding experience.

How to get clients? To begin with, offer services to friends, also watch the society pages for announcements of engagements. Once you are successfully launched, word of mouth recommendations will probably keep you busy.

The Cash Flow:

This enterprise can be carried on from home, obviating rent expense. Except for postage on letters in a possible mail campaign, your budget should be a small one.

What to charge is a problem, but one such service begins by charging $25 an hour for consultation and planning and then has a minimum fee of $300 and a maximum of $2,000.

BEAUTICIAN AT HOME

The Idea:

On a cross-country drive, it is not unusual to see a sign in the window or on the lawn of a house in a residential section proclaiming that a beautician is within. Here is a woman who works at home, need not go out in bad weather, and has the operation of her house only a wall away.

Getting Started:

If this line of work appeals to you, the first thing is to learn the techniques of hair care, styling and dressing, make-up counseling, and hand and nail care. This is usually done through a course of study at an appropriate school. Then at least a short term of actual experience in a beauty parlor certainly won't come amiss. Much can be learned in the way of setting up appointments, customer relations, keeping accounts, the ways of publicity, and all the details of running a specialized business.

When you are ready to open, send out personal letters to as many women as you can list. Have small cards printed with the name, address, and telephone number of your place of business, with "By Appointment" in the left hand corner, and keep these cards on your appointment desk, as well as planting them in as many neighborhood business establishments as will accept them. Take ads in newspapers and in local papers, like church periodicals. The latter reach women living nearby and do not cost much. If there are local radio and television stations near, contact them and take an ad. Announce special reductions for the first twenty customers. Make as much as you can of your opening.

The Cash Flow:

This is a fairly expensive project and you may have to

seek a bank loan. (See Chapter II.) The courses of study at beauty culture schools, and their prices, vary from school to school and in different parts of the country. At a standard school in New York, the time is six and a half months, full time, or fourteen months if you go part-time in the evenings. The price for either course is $1,490.

You will have to prepare the part of the house you mean to devote to your work and make it ready to receive the necessary equipment: hydraulic chair, wet unit, hair driers, manicure table and chair. These can probably be ordered through your school or possibly obtained second hand. There is also the continuing expense of rollers, pins, lotions, sprays. These need a movable caddy.

You might need to partition your business section from your living quarters and, almost certainly, you will require plumbing adjustments.

The zoning laws should be checked by your lawyer.

Advertising and publicity budget is not small and is necessary to keep your business before your public in this competitive field.

However, there are millions of beauty customers, coast to coast, and if yours is the only beauty parlor within several blocks or more, and if you publicize yourself properly, you should draw people, certainly in the opening days. After that, your own expertise, plus friendly but businesslike administration should carry you on.

As for charges, if you have worked in a beauty shop, you know the going rate for your locality. If not, find out what others are charging.

ENTERTAINMENT BUREAU

The Idea:

The group promotion of entertainers has grown into a profitable business for a young woman in a middle-sized city. She drew up a list of locals in the entertainment field—band leaders, dancers, drama clubs, and so forth—got in touch with them and offered to send out promotional letters to nearby clubs, religious groups, and charitable organizations that have fund-raising programs. This has worked well.

Getting Started:

If you feel you would like to initiate a similar activity in your town or city, you need, first, to know your field, both the entertainers and those to be entertained. Your performers will probably be local, good enough to be professional and ask pay for their appearances but not well enough known to be on the list of national booking managements. Your bureau will take artists who are between the amateur and the big pro status.

Another vital quality for the booking agent is a highly developed sense of people, a feeling for bringing suitable elements together. If the Board of Governors of the local private school is putting on a dinner dance, they probably want a band that can play fox trots and waltzes, with an occasional rhumba, not the hottest rock group in town. The hottest rock group, however, might be just what the J.D.'s and their gals would go for. Religious organizations might like the drama club in a musicale, like "Brigadoon," or a hardy perennial comedy like "The Women." The entertainment should fit the audience.

The Cash Flow:

If you have typewriter, desk, and filing cabinet space available, you can work from home, or, if a business address seems more impressive, perhaps inexpensive desk space (see

Yellow Pages under "Office and Desk Space Rental Service"), with mailing address, and switchboard service can be obtained in a well-located building.

Mailing lists will be of the utmost importance to you; every new club or other organization should be carefully added with names of its officers. Special stationery should be ordered; consult with the printer on an effective heading. Your correspondence will be heavy, letters to promote and to arrange dates and fees, and a big telephone bill will be another running expense.

Some managements ask an initial sum for taking on an artist, others are satisfied with commissions on appearances.

TRAVEL SLIDES AND LECTURES

The Idea

Who has not spent an evening trying hard to keep awake while a neighbor shows slides of a trip to a national playground, to California, or to Europe? The pictures are mostly of himself or his spouse and offspring, feeding the pigeons in St. Mark's Square, eyeing the bears in Yellowstone Park, or about to climb into the recesses of the Statue of Liberty.

However, there is another type of slides, taken more objectively and featuring the beauty of landscape, building or historic room, of church or cathedral; or showing the spectacle of a great horse or marine race, the entrants and the colorful crowds. This kind of slides can almost make the viewer feel as if he were on the scene.

Taking such slides is a highly developed skill, calling for a natural flair for color and balance in a picture and a cultivated knowledge of light, distance, timing, and other phases of photography.

If you have such a talent, and have built up a sufficient

library of slides that you wish to show for gain, you also need to be a good commentator, with clear and pleasant diction. You need a carefully written script to go with the slides, giving pertinent facts in an entertaining manner, with the information condensed into the short space of time your slide is on the screen.

Your slides need not be of travel. You can have other specialties, like birds or animals, trees of different regions, gardens in rural, suburban, city, or historic settings, interiors of country mansions, castles in Spain and elsewhere, contrast in dwellings of the affluent and the underprivileged, special types of architecture—the possibilities are legion.

Getting Started:

Perhaps you had better find your feet by giving your programs gratis to your schools or community groups. In this way you will learn affinity with your audiences, as well as how to coordinate your slide showing with your comments. If technical difficulties arise, for instance, if an occasional slide comes upside down or there is a mechanical failure, you must learn to cope. You must also learn to time your program accurately. If it is supposed to be an hour and a half, with intermission, don't run over. If you share a program with another entertainer, keep to your time limit.

Next, you might *try* to get on the list of entertainers of an established lecture bureau. (Consult the Yellow Pages.) Chances are that you will have to wait for such connection until you are established yourself.

Get a list of clubs, schools, colleges, religious and charitable organizations that might be interested in your programs. Write to them, describing what you have to offer. If you can afford it, have a brochure designed and produced by your local printer, giving your background and featuring a few reproductions of some of your most intriguing slides. Quote terms and give your address in the brochure. If you must travel to keep engagements, try to schedule the appearances as near together as possible, avoiding long jumps between them.

The Cash Flow:

It may be some time before this activity earns you a living, but if you can afford it as part-time work at first it may develop into a well-paying project. Your mail campaign and brochure will amount to several hundred dollars as an initial expense and the letters will be a continuing expense, since you should send them out at least once a year. Ads in magazines appropriate to your specialty are good, if your budget stretches that far. Your fee must be high enough to cover travel expenses and other items and leave a reasonable profit. Calculate overall expenses and leave yourself 50% to 75% profit on each engagement. Or you can quote a flat fee with the understanding that your travel expenses will be additional, which is all right for single appearances but does not work if you have a tour.

If and when your name gets on the list of a good lecture agency, some of your troubles should be over. There are people in this field, though, who think they do a better booking job for themselves than any agency can.

MUSIC STUDIO

The Idea:

To operate a music studio you need a background of special knowledge and training, of course, But let us say that you are skilled'in playing several instruments, the piano, and perhaps guitar and accordion, and that you have completed studies in harmony, theory, and sight reading. Then, provided you add to these qualifications patience and ability to teach, why not open a music center in your own home? You can give lessons in the instruments you know, perhaps team up with musically inclined friends who can teach other instruments. A

community and/or children's chorus can interest people of a
wide age range, give them a fascinating, productive hobby,
call introverts out of their isolation, and generally promote
good spirits and satisfaction in achievement.

Getting Started:

Number one requirement, a good piano. Number two,
space enough to accommodate a large group of people. If you
have those, plus your own talents, then contact your local
music store or stores, both the piano and instrument stores,
and the record shops. Ask them to help you by spreading the
word to their customers, especially on the chorus, and letting
you leave printed announcement cards on their premises.
Since activities like yours help their business, they will
probably cooperate. Advertise in the local press, on radio and
in the Yellow Pages.

After you have taught for some months, begin to give
programs, perhaps small ones featuring two good pupils at a
time. Spur on your choristers, adult and juvenile, with the
prospect of a Christmas or spring concert. Let the members
contribute to the expenses and form committees to carry out
such tasks as choosing the auditorium for the concert,
deciding whether or not the concert will be an invitation affair
or with tickets sold for the benefit of some charity. Do
everything you can to promote the feeling of commitment and
involvement.

The Cash Flow:

Advertising will be your main expense if you work from
home. Your individual lessons should be charged at $5 to $10
per hour. The fee for each child in the youngster's chorus
might be $20 for a season of eight weeks, with weekly training
sessions, perhaps on Saturday mornings. Adult choristers
might pay $25 for eight weeks, assembling for training weekly,
in the evening.

DRAMA CLASSES

Which of us does not feel that in her the stage lost a great actress? Children act, from the cradle, and many an octogenarian has dramatized his last breath. The urge for drama is universal, admitted or not. Prehistoric people probably acted with grunts and pantomime.

A way to capitalize on this widespread trait is to offer an outlet in the study of drama and acting. Classes for children, young adults and their seniors can bring interest to both teachers and pupils and can be developed into a paying proposition. Plays and playlets can be put on and—with time and success—a Little Theatre and a local season can be fostered.

Getting Started:

Of course, you don't just wake up some morning and decide to be a drama teacher. Some kind of background is necessary to make people accept your authority and respect your direction. Have you ever trod the boards in summer stock, in college, in a recognized Little Theatre group? If you were not in the cast, were you director, assistant director, stage manager, lighting technician, set designer, or costumer in any of these? Did you ever attend drama classes yourself, under some well-known teacher? If you can produce some experience that indicates knowledge of the stage, then you can expect to attract pupils and begin your project.

The classes can be held in your home. You need some impressive books of your own to form your library (if you are interested in this field, you probably have a large assortment already). You need a textbook to teach from and your pupils need copies, which they buy for themselves. Same with scripts. If you can type, it will be a great help in preparing material, cue sheets, and the like.

To begin, you probably know several people who want to study with you. They will tell friends and your student group will grow. You might advertise in neighborhood publications and put announcement cards on bulletin boards, but satisfied students are your best promotion.

When you begin to produce plays, you need a production staff, as well as actors, and some people are quite happy manipulating lighting or making costumes, rather than appearing on stage. Above all, have a reliable stage manager, or else take that important assignment yourself, as well as the directing. Among the stage manager's many responsibilities is seeing that props are *where* they ought to be *when* they ought to be. It can be a disaster if the heroine rushes in to snatch a letter from the table to flourish in the villain's face—and the letter is not there!

The Cash Flow:

To set up this activity takes little money. Your courses should be something like 10 or 20 lessons, given twice a week, for about $25 or $50 a student, depending on how many lessons. If you have 10, or even five students in a class, that is not bad, since you will have several classes, according to age and advancement.

When you start producing, be very sure you understand the royalty involved, if any, before you decide on a play.

PUPPET THEATRE

The Idea:

About the most mobile stock company possible is a puppet troupe that, unlike human actors, can be packed in relatively small space and transported, with no problems of food and lodging. Puppets, while they can present their own kind of difficulties, such as tangled strings, are not temperamental and, if handled correctly, will obey direction unquestioningly.

The puppet theatre, found in many countries around the world, has an appeal that has survived the centuries. Current puppet attractions range from those for children, that is, the animal, fantasy, and fairy tale figures, to adult entertainment in night clubs and theatres, even in opera. Several years ago puppets arrived from Salzburg and toured in Mozart works.

Getting Started:

If you want to be a puppeteer, the first thing, of course, is to learn—learn to make puppets and to gauge their possibilities and your own as their master; to study this repertoire and write your own dialogue or adapt someone else's; to assume several voices; to costume the puppets; to give them, and your own special show, individuality and character.

At the Wallace Lee Puppet Studio in New York, beginning training is in four steps: (1) model puppet in clay; (2) make a mold from plaster of paris; (3) cast the puppet, pouring either plastic wood or latex in the mold; (4) sandpaper the head. There are various types of puppets: the hand or glove puppet; the marionette or string puppet; the shadow puppet; the stick puppet (made on a stick). Courses at this studio are eight weeks, with three-hour lessons either once or twice a week. Lectures set forth the technique of staging puppet shows and the students are required to write and deliver dialogue. Some modern puppeteers tape their dialogue, using several voices, but this is not traditional. How long should a puppeteer study? A difficult question. This is an art and you are never done learning.

But when you believe you are ready, you can try for engagements with your puppets, on lecture and concert courses, in schools and colleges, libraries, museums, before clubs. Department stores, especially at Christmas time, sometimes put on puppet shows for the children. A New England couple, where the wife makes the puppets and the husband writes script and manipulates them, travel in their station wagon, giving performances over a wide territory.

Besides touring, you can open your own teaching studio. People of all ages find self-expression in making puppets.

The Cash Flow:

Income varies. A few puppeteers get big fees, but most of them count puppeteering as a part-time activity. The New England couple mentioned gets $35 a performance, not a large return when you consider transportation and living costs for two on tour.

But the fascination is great and the little creations do brighten the life of a puppeteer.

ANTIQUE SHOP

The Idea:

Dealing in antiques is a business which can start little and grow big, depending on how much time you want to devote to it. Some people pick up likely, and salable, items, refinish and refurbish them at leisure, and then either keep them if they like them that well or sell them when a customer turns up. On the other hand, the real zealot works hard, scouring the locality for choice pieces, which are all bound for sale for profit after they are restored.

Speaking of restoration, before you enter this business, you should be confident of your skill and patience as a restorer. Museums often give courses in restoring old furniture and a period of working, in this and other ways, with an established antique dealer is a canny preliminary.

Getting Started:

You need to think of your neighborhood and vicinity. Are there already so many antique stores that a new one can hardly flourish? Which sort of shop would be most likely to succeed, the kind that is really a second-hand shop, with all sorts of furniture and bric-a-brac acquired regardless of period or style, or the more specialized and sophisticated type, devoted to early American, Victorian, English, French, or Italian pieces? The first kind is a lot easier, and if you do not want to take pains with your decor, but push everything together in the middle of the floor, some customers like it that way. If they delve into a mass of objects and come up with a painted fan or an old glass goblet, they feel the thrill of discovery.

For the second kind of shop, you need to space the pieces, in both window and interior, and have a plan of effective display, the arrangement suitable to the period and country you wish to suggest.

In either case, you should choose your location carefully, where plenty of people walk or drive past. Some successful antique shops are in rural areas where rents are low, *but* are where their sign can be seen by passing motorists.

Advertising here takes careful study and should be in publications that your customers read. Sunday papers are good, also club and neighborhood magazines and programs of local events, like theatrical productions, concerts, horse shows.

The Cash Flow:

To begin, you need money for your stock, and of course you always plan for replacements. You probably will tour a lot in your station wagon, running down pieces you have heard of and attending country auctions and estate sales, so gas and upkeep is a factor. Mailing lists are important for direct mail and must be kept up to date and added to.

Rent is part of the budget, unless you are lucky enough to live in the country and have an old barn near the highway that you can convert into a shop.

Mark-up between the price paid for a piece and its sale after restoration has to be high, considering all the time that good restoration takes, so furniture usually carries big prices. Sometimes there are small objects that perhaps came with an estate purchase that can be less costly and thus move fast.

SHOPPING GUIDE FOR OUT-OF-TOWNERS

The Idea:

Most women like to shop. One of them has made it pay in instead of paying out. A resident of a major city, she guides out-of-towners to the right exclusive boutique for clothes, shoes, furs, jewelry, glassware, china, bric-a-brac. Shop owners are glad to pay her a commission. On the other hand, the client pays her if she is asked to arrange a theatre, dining program; a cultural day or evening at museums, concert, or opera; or even take a group on a Sunday walking tour to some of the city's historical or beauty spots.

Getting Started:

How did she get clients and establish herself? To begin with, she had many out-of-town acquaintainces and would show them around the bazaars and pleasure spots just for friendship and to amuse herself. Then one of the shop owners spoke to her, offering her commissions. It made her think. She visited other shops and got them to make a similar agreement. Then she wrote to her friends, telling them frankly that she was going into business as a shopping guide, asking for their patronage and their recommendation to other shoppers. Of course, her service did not cost her friends anything, the shops paid the commissions. Her clientele grew.

Next, she contacted convention bureaus, suggesting her guidance for visiting wives and/or children, outlining a day's sightseeing or a theatre and supper evening, suited to all ages and tastes. For these days or evenings, she asks a fee and expenses.

The Cash Flow:

Her expenses are almost non-existent, since she does not advertise. She has a mailing list, but seldom sends out any form letters, preferring to write individually to each person.

The shops pay her a commission of 10% on purchases made by her clients. Her fee for a day's or evening's guidance to sightseeing or entertainment is from $20 for a half day to $35 for a full day, and $25 for an evening.

5.

RESEARCH IS THE NAME OF THE GAME

RESEARCH FOR AUTHORS

The Idea:

Do you know any writers of novels? If you do, you know that, as Frank Swinnerton, who in his day was one of the most successful of the breed, wrote feelingly, "novelists are expected to be walking encyclopedias." If the novelist makes a mistake, in a quotation, in a point of law, or in a historical date, some reader is sure to catch the inaccuracy. Therefore, novelists—ditto playwrights—keep as error-free as they can. This involves much time-consuming research.

Here, then, is where a person who likes research, and has the time to devote to it, can find interesting assignments. If you are such a person, if you enjoy research which might range from historical data to medical lore, from geographical location to an appropriate menu for a dinner party in England in 1848, then you should try to contact as many busy fiction writers as you can and offer your help.

Getting Started:

How to contact them? Run an ad in the writers' trade magazines, like *The Writer* and *Writers Digest*. Write to publishers' and authors' agents stressing your abilities, and your experience when you have gained some, and ask them to recommend you to their authors. Write to the authors themselves, care of their publishers. One assignment well carried off will lead to others.

The Cash Flow:

Your advertising and your letters describing your service will probably be a continuing expense.

Probably your charge will be by the hour, perhaps $5, or you might consult with the client beforehand and agree on a flat fee, based on how readily available or how obscure the research in question might be.

SCHOOL ADVISORY SERVICE

The Idea:

Do you know puzzled parents who want to put their offspring in private school but are not sure which one? If you do—and almost everyone does know such pondering progenitors—it may lead you to consider a needed service. That of school advisor.

There are many types of private schools today, all specialized to meet different needs. Schools on elementary, intermediate, and college levels; trade and technical schools; schools for the physically or mentally handicapped, the dropout, or the gifted youngster. In the summer, we have camps for the sports-loving child or the musical child, or drama camps, sailing camps, riding camps, fishing camps. How are parents even to know about all of them, let alone select one that best fits the needs of their children?

Getting Started:

Here's where the school advisor can step in and provide information. *Note:* The advisor provides information, not recommendations. The former requires no prior qualifications or license; the latter may. Check with your lawyer.

Here is a suggested plan for beginning: Compile a list of all private schools in your area from telephone and school directories. Next, visit each of them and contact the principal, dean, or registration officer, and outline your plan of meeting with parents and informing them about schools. If a referral comes from you to the school, you are entitled to a commission of 10% of a year's tuition (this is customary with most schools). Since your plan involves no payment on the school's part until you actually send them a pupil, it is likely that you and the school will agree on this.

The Cash Flow:

Advertising will be the greater part of your expense. An ad in the Yellow Pages under "Schools Advisory Service" will probably be productive, and a direct mail (letters to parents) and telephone campaign can help build up a clientele.

The intake will vary. If you send a family of four children to an expensive day school, your bank balance will escalate. You cannot count on such a bonanza too often, but most private schools are fairly costly and a steady stream of students to many types of schools will reward steady efforts. And this is a "people" business, fine for those who like to meet and talk to their fellow citizens.

STAMP COLLECTORS' BOOKLET

The Idea:

If you are a stamp collector yourself, or if someone in your family has this hobby and shares his joys and frustrations with you, there is a way you can put this knowledge to work.

Get out a pamphlet listing current values of stamps. Also include the names and addresses of firms interested in purchasing collections of stamps. If you keep strictly up to date and bring out your booklet monthly, it should be valuable to stamp fanciers who must stay abreast of all developments in their field. The subscribers could, of course, get all this information for themselves from the same sources you consult, but you offer it to them assembled and coordinated. You get the data yourself from a local philatelic club, by thorough research through the post office and public library, and by subscribing to stamp catalogs and the philatelic trade papers.

How to produce this booklet? Type the information neatly in appropriate sections on regular typewriter paper. Mimeograph or Xerox the sheets and staple them together. Plan your pamphlet to run from 16 to 24 pages per issue.

Getting Started:

To get subscribers, run a small ad in newspapers, especially the Sunday magazine sections, and in the leading stamp journals. Ask members of your philatelic club to tell their associates about your service.

The Cash Flow:

You will need to subscribe to a good many periodicals, such as *Stamps*, Holley, New York, *The Philatelic Journal*, New York City, *Western Stamp Collector*, Albany, Oregon. If you are a collector yourself, you probably know them all; if not, the Ayers Directory in your public library lists them. You need the catalogs of stamp dealers, big and little. Your advertising, at least at the beginning, should be as extensive as you can afford. Advertising will be a continuing expense but can diminish to some degree as your subscription list builds up and there are a substantial number of renewals to count on.

This is a valuable, specialized service, so you can charge as high as $15 a copy for your booklet. Then if you calculate on an initial printing of, say, 100 copies, your budget might run something like this: 24-page booklet, cost ($3 per page) $72 for 100 copies. Add $200 for advertising, postage, and miscellaneous expenses. If you receive $15 a copy, this gives a gross profit of $1500 (on 100 copies) and approximately $1,000 net.

HANDWRITING ANALYSIS

The Idea:

Does handwriting reveal character? Many people believe it does. Graphologists are employed in some personnel departments to give their opinion on the psychological make-up of applicants for jobs.

If you have studied graphology as a hobby, or are interested in the study of this subject, you could eventually turn a profit from your knowledge. How to obtain such knowledge? Books on graphology are to be found in the public library which embody the principles of the science.

Getting Started:

After you feel that your study has brought you expertise, you can practice on your friends and then progress to offering your services at parties. In these contacts you will not only develop quickness and ease in analysis but you will perceive the value of tact. Whatever horrendous subsurface traits the handwriting of an acquaintance may reveal, you can hardly shout it out at a party!

When you are thoroughly experienced, insert a small ad in your newspaper and begin to go pro. Ask each client to submit a specimen of his handwriting, along with his age, place of birth, and present occupation. The treatise you prepare for him should be about 500 words in length, fully analyzing his handwriting and suggesting basic aptitudes and where self-improvement is indicated. Again, tact is vital. Accentuate the positive!

After some months of experience of this kind, you might see the editor of a newspaper and offer to do a column on graphology. Here is an opportunity for a regular income, week in and week out, which would not interfere with your individual clients.

The Cash Flow:

This work can certainly be done at home, obviating rent, and with no great increase in the telephone bill, although postage and stationery costs must be counted in this budget, as well as your advertising, modest but constant.

For individual consultations, a suggested charge is $25. The fee for the newspaper column will have to be negotiated.

CASTING HOROSCOPES

The Idea:

Don't say casting horoscopes is just for kooks. Some of the greatest leaders and highest-powered brains in history have looked to the stars for guidance. An individually cast horoscope, drawn up by an expert astrologer, costs a bundle and is a far cry from the one you can buy along with your evening paper. To prepare a horoscope properly is time-consuming, hard, concentrated work, involving the skilled use of charts and considerable knowledge of the vital statistics of a client, such as the exact time of his birth and what the relevant stars were doing at that moment.

Getting Started:

Aspiring astrologers who need to begin by seeking schooling, can find informative books in the public libraries. The Yellow Pages of many city telephone directories list instruction in the ancient art. New York's Yellow Pages devotes more than two columns to "astrologers," including schools, classes, and teachers, as well as counseling.

After a reasonable course of study has been completed, it is a good idea for a neophyte to get experience by obliging at parties and volunteering to read horoscopes at fund-raising affairs.

Then comes advertising in the publications most likely to be seen by prospective clients, like local newspapers, neighborhood publications, theatre and other programs. Word of mouth is, as always, a strong promotional factor. As expertise increases, the astrologer can begin to advertise in national publications.

The Cash Flow:

This is a business that can be, and usually is, conducted from home. However, some astrologers whose scope is extensive enough work from offices. The pay can be high. One Middle Western woman gets $125 and up for casting a horoscope, although, of course, many of her colleagues are satisfied with the $5 to $50 range.

HELP WRITE THESES

The Idea:

If you have had experience as a writer and editor or as a teacher of English, and if you are good at organizing a mass of material into a coherent article or treatise, you can give a rescuing hand to students and graduate students who are faced with writing a thesis for a Masters or Ph.D. degree. Some of these students, of course, are more than able to author their'theses for themselves, but others, well versed in their subjects and with a wealth of pertinent facts on hand, just do not have the gift of making intelligent and interesting order out of a chaos of details and references.

It is unethical and unfair to all concerned for you to actually write the thesis, but there is nothing wrong with your meeting with the candidate, discussing the subject and the phase of it being written about, and working with the student toward proper arrangement, sequence, emphasis, climax, and conclusion. Must you be an authority on the subject? Not necessarily. Unless the terminology is so technical as to be unintelligible to a layman, you can tell when ideas are clarifying and the whole thought process taking shape. Your part is to do a lot of listening. Making everything clear to you helps the student shape his own mental conceptions. You can suggest and help with further research and exclude repetitions.

Study of finished theses is advisable on your part so that you are familiar with the form, how the references are keyed, and how constant is the reliance on references.

Writing a thesis is a serious business, and many interviews between you and the student will no doubt be necessary. Probably the two of you will first hold discussions, then work out an outline, showing the structure of the composition with its beginning, middle, and end, and the ramifications of the chief and subsidiary points. Then the references can be assembled and the writing begin. By this time the student should find it easier to put the material in proper wording. Finally, a complete thesis has evolved, clear in purpose, well worded, and with the thrust of its original idea strong and effective.

Getting Started:

If this is new work for you, perhaps you had better try your skill without pay on some close friend or family member. Then when you are confident of your ability, ask your original student to tell the story in scholastic circles, to students and professors alike. Put cards describing your service on the college bulletin boards. If you take a small ad in the college paper, this is good public relations, besides bringing your service before the student body.

The Cash Flow:

In this job, the amount of time you devote to a student is more of a tax than the small amount of money going for advertising, but fees should not be low. If you charge at least $5 an hour and a student comes for 20 2-hour sessions, that brings the bill to $200. If the thought of paying by the hour makes your client nervous, quote a flat fee based on the time you estimate will be required.

LIBRARY CATALOGUING

The Idea:

A moonlighting librarian in the Middle West has augmented her income by cataloguing the libraries of a number of citizens of her town. These people, like many of us, had accumulated books over the years, some inherited, some purchased new, some bought in bulk at auctions. Thus there were, in these private libraries, a large conglomeration of books, placed at random on the shelves. To find a specific book, or even to know what books were available, involved time and search.

Owners of book collections like this were glad to pay the enterprising librarian a good fee for her time in bringing order out of chaos and enabling them to check an orderly record and go straight to a required volume.

Getting Started:

News of such a service should be spread over as wide an area as you can encompass by traveling in your car, returning home the same day. This calls for composing a small ad and inserting it in the newspapers of the vicinity. A short, recurrent ad on local radio stations might also bring results. You can visit public libraries and book stores and tell about what you can do and ask that the word be passed on to people who might be clients. Leave your name, address, and telephone number.

If you are a librarian or have had library training, the work of sorting out a private library will probably be simple for you. If you do not have such a background, try separating the books into categories, like Fiction, Poetry, Philosophy, Biography, History, Science. If there is a lot of fiction, perhaps you should divide it into Classic and Contemporary.

List each category alphabetically according to authors; make a file card for each title and arrange these cards in file boxes or drawers, each category having its own drawer or space.

Then arrange the books on the shelves, category by category, alphabetically by author. If the shelves are irregular in size and shape, you may encounter problems in this orderly plan, since books are not of uniform size either. Such problems must be worked out individually. Just keep in mind that the arrangement on the shelves must agree with the arrangement of the file cards.

The Cash Flow:

All this entails quite a lot of work, especially if there are several hundred books. A fair charge may be $12 to $15 an hour. Expenses include ads and gas for your car.

TRANSLATING BUREAU

The Idea:

If you are lucky enough to be proficient in a foreign language, there are many ways of taking advantage of your skill, financially speaking. One way is to set up your own translating bureau. Now that communications have made the world so much smaller and commercial and social exchange between nations has increased so greatly, there is a demand for translation of letters, business and personal; of articles and scientific treatises; of novels and short stories for publishers. If you not only write but speak the second language well, you can assist at business conferences as an interpreter and, sometimes you may have all expenses paid, and a fee added, when you guide sightseeing, shopping, or theatre tours for non-English speaking visitors.

Getting Started:

Before you open your own business, you might consider working for one of the big translating bureaus. Such experience gives you valuable background for selling your own services.

When you are ready to start on your own, advertisements in newspapers, both those in English and in the second language, are a means of getting clients. Even more effective than advertising are recommendations of your bureau from associate to associate and from friend to friend.

A business like this can be carried on from home, but perhaps it is better to have a business address for your sort of work. By consulting the Yellow Pages under "Office and Desk Rental Service," you will find offers of desk space, mailing address, and switchboard service.

The Cash Flow:

Expenses for this project are relatively low. If you work from home, you have no rent. If you favor the desk space rental arrangement, these costs are not high. Advertising, telephone charges, stationery, and postage are included in the budget.

Fee for translation ranges from $5 to $15 a page, depending on extensiveness.

TUTORING

The Idea:

Children of elementary and grade school age often need

the boost in their studies that a tutor can give, and so do their older siblings in high school and college.

If tutoring work attracts you, you are probably a person who likes and understands the young. Patience is the operative word, of course. A child or young person who needs tutoring obviously has a problem. Can you dig into each case and help the youngster to either get over the snag or be referred to the right kind of help—medical or psychological? Many times the child is only lazy or bored. If the subject is made interesting by the tutor, all may be well.

Do you prefer working with children or with young adults? What are your own best subjects? Both you and your students will be happier if you enjoy your work.

Getting Started:

How to begin? Try first to get students from among your own acquaintances. If they do well, they and their parents will tell others.

Typed announcements should go on the bulletin boards of schools, colleges, and community centers. Small ads placed in your local newspaper and Yellow Pages can be effective, and don't neglect to take an ad in the school paper, if there is one.

The Cash Flow:

Most tutors charge by the hour—$5 to $10—or you can make a rate for a specified period, like one or two months, with four hours tutoring a week, or whatever schedule the student requires. Your chief expense is your advertising. If you prefer to work with students in your own home, this does away with transportation costs. If you go to the students, you must allow for carfare or gasoline.

GENEALOGICAL RESEARCH

The Idea:

Search for identity is a lifelong preoccupation with all of us. A manifestation of such search very common in the United States of the 20th century is a burning curiosity to learn more about our forebears. In fact, some cite genealogy as the third most popular hobby of Americans.

There are many reasons for looking up your ancestors, near and remote. First, just to find out more of who you are and what made you. Then perhaps you want to join the DAR, the Colonial Dames, the Mayflower Society, the Daughters of 1812, or one of the many other historical organizations. This kind of search usually ends on this side of the Atlantic, but not always. Some of our fellow citizens claim to trace their lineage back to Charlemagne.

Adopted children often seek knowledge of their biological parents. Another and very practical reason for obtaining proof of descent is for an individual to establish himself as an heir to money or property left in a will to the descendants of some certain person. Then there is the scientific viewpoint. Eugenicists are interested in genealogy because through such findings they can sometimes trace a physical characteristic or weakness and add to their understanding of heredity.

Getting Started:

To enter this fascinating but exacting profession, you should take stock of your own personality, inherited or not. Are you precise, do you examine a fact from all angles to determine not only its authenticity but its bearing on the subject in hand? Have you patience—and the eyesight—to pore over old letters and documents in handwriting and script of another day? Can you scrutinize a romantic tradition and debunk it, if necessary, in the interests of truth? Can you be tireless in searching out and consulting public records, family

Bibles, photographs and correspondence, tombstone inscriptions?

If your answer is yes to all these questions, then you might take out from the public library some books on genealogy, like "Genealogical Research, Methods and Sources," put out by the American Society of Genealogists, this to precede taking a course in the work. Universities and colleges, in the adult education courses, often include genealogy. Some YWCA's teach it and you can study individually with a recognized genealogist. For suggestions for study, consult your State Historical Society, whose address you can find in your public library.

Then when you are ready for business perhaps you have clients waiting. If you want more, you can advertise in such professional journals as The Genealogical Helper, 526 North Main Street, Logan, Utah 84321, and the Genealogical Books in Print, 6818 Lois Drive, Springfield, Va. 22150. Both are usually in public libraries and consulted by eager searchers after ancestors, as well as by other genealogists.

The Cash Flow:

The genealogical courses take several weeks. They are relatively inexpensive and so are the small ads. Your headquarters can be your own home. As for your fees, a genealogist of national reputation suggests $5 an hour as standard charge. If you have a determined and well-heeled client, you may have to travel and have your expenses paid when you go to a distant point to follow up a clue. If the client is not so affluent, you may enlist the services of a colleague who is on the spot, for instance, in Washington, D.C., if the search is to be in, say, the National Archives. Before you run up expenses by travel or consultation, be sure to contact the nearest Mormon Church and find out if one of their Stake Libraries is in reach. In these centers are microfilms of a vast number of materials relevant to genealogy and if they do not have the ones you need they will send away to another Stake Library and borrow them for you.

6.

FOR THE CREATIVE-MINDED

FLOWER ARRANGING

The Idea:

A flair for design, with emphasis on line and grace, can be expressed with flowers. If you have such a flair and have developed a skill in arranging blooms and branches, there are ways to make this talent pay in money as well as pleasure. The established flower arranger can charge for decorating for luncheons, banquets, private parties, weddings, hotel lobbies. Striking floral arrangements—like espaliered branches along the wall, or a tropical isle in the center—can make a charity ball memorable. Classes in flower arrangement can be lucrative; also lectures before clubs and educational institutions.

Getting Started:

There are many schools of floral arrangement, such as the traditional (or Williamsburg), the Victorian, the contemporary, etc. Study of one or several of these can be carried on through books from the Public Library and, most important, by membership in a club affiliated with the Federated Garden Clubs of U.S.A. The club will have informative meetings and lectures by flower arrangers advanced in the field. Another valuable aid is the magazine issued by the Federation.

Very popular in the world's flower scene is the Japanese art of Ikebana. This type of floral expression came to Japan centuries ago from China and has been developed into an integral part of Japanese culture, involving history, philosophy, and mysticism as potent influences on the individual flower creation. Ikebana is taught worldwide by several schools, including Ikenobo, which is the oldest, Ohara, Sugetso, and many more. All have literature, lectures, and teaching headquarters and can be contacted through your club. In Ikebana, the effects are made with only a few flowers and other materials, as opposed to western flower arrangement, which usually calls for masses of bloom.

Before you go professional, you should have entered a number of qualified flower shows and have an impressive collection of ribbons for winning exhibits. These ribbons, incidentally, will not be for Ikebana arrangements. Ikebana has shows but awards no prizes.

The Cash Flow:

The training for a career as a flower arranger can be expensive, involving fees for courses, the price of publications, and club membership. In Ikebana there are grades of scholarship. Some occidental Ikebana students go to Japan to receive advanced degrees.

Word of mouth is the best publicity for paying engagements. The flower world is farflung, embracing almost all western countries, but it is a tight little world, too. Endorsement for a new professional comes best from the qualified inner circle. However, you can also advertise in local news-papers and perhaps in the magazines of fraternal orders that give balls and banquets.

Charges? Lectures can bring $75 and up, with expenses; classes $5 to $10 per student per lesson in a course of, say, twelve sessions. For decorations for gala occasions, the fees can range widely, from $100 for a small wedding to several thousand dollars for a major civic banquet.

DRIED FLOWER ART

The Idea:

When you shop the fine gift sections of the best depart-ment stores, you see pictures made from dried flowers and leaves glued to a white or tinted background, framed in narrow gold. Obviously the work of someone skilled in flower craft and endowed with a feeling for design and color, they are expensive and are treasured for wedding gifts, gifts for the woman who has everything—that sort of thing.

An artist who creates them needs basic artistic skill, along with knowledge of the old-fashioned art of drying flowers.

Getting Started:

If this sort of self-expression attracts you, almost any public library can furnish books of instruction, and craft centers frequently include such training in their curricula. Collecting and drying flowers entails gathering the blooms in season, going out into the woods and marshes in search of "dry material" (seeds, pods, and dried twigs and foliage) at the right time of year, and giving it all the correct treatment. Not easy. Takes an interested, even dedicated person.

When the materials are ready, the flowers pressed and dried, the leaves and other dry material prepared, you apply selected pieces to a design you have prepared on cardboard, silk, felt, or linen with a special glue, let it dry, and insert the picture in its frame. Besides pictures, you can make paperweights, trays, medallions, greeting cards, and so on.

When you have such items prepared you are ready to find a market. One lady, skilled in dried flower art, made up a representative selection and ventured into New York's exclusive Bergdorf-Goodman store. She was referred to the manager, who was ready with the courteous brushoff. However, he *did* glance at her wares. Now Bergdorf and other stores take all the pieces she can turn out.

You can make a similar contact, going in person to a store or shop that you believe would be interested. You can also take individual orders.

The Cash Flow:

Due to the time consumed in this work, it probably offers a better way to supplement an income than to constitute a living. However, for individual orders, you can charge $15 for your paperweights, $35 to $50 for pictures or trays, depending on the size and on your market. When your fame spreads, you can hold classes, charging about $5 an hour per pupil.

This is home work, so there would be no rent. The flowers can come from your own or a neighbor's garden, the dried material from the woods. The cardboard or fabric for backgrounds, the glass forms for the paperweights and trays are your chief expense.

LANDSCAPE AND GARDEN PLANNING

The Idea:

Have you a garden that is a showplace for your neighborhood? Is it planned so that each season brings its own glories of color and design? If so, you undoubtedly have learned the qualities of the soil of your locality, which plants, flowers, and shrubs grow best, their rate of growth, blooming period, and special care necessary.

Why not develop an interesting business from this knowledge and ability? Become a lawn and garden consultant. In these days when so many couples are moving from city to suburb, you should have plenty of people eager for your service. Look at any middle income development and note when the house is up and ready for occupancy, how bare, treeless, and shrubless is the sparse lawn. The ex-city dweller moving in probably knows nothing about gardening and landscaping in general, let alone the local soil and climate.

Getting Started:

Professional landscape architects take long training, but they usually are called in on much bigger assignments and draw a much larger fee than yours, and so offer you little or no competition. In preparing to start, have colored pictures taken of your garden in its seasonal phases, put them in an attractive album and have it ready to take with you and show. Tell everyone you know what you plan to do, especially builders and real estate agents. Take ads in the Yellow Pages and on the gardening pages of newspapers.

When you survey the lawn and spaces assigned to gardens, you, as an experienced and creative gardener, can visualize what shrubbery and trees are called for, what borders and beds of which flowers would be most appropriate. You should draw a plan for your client, water color sketches, if possible, ranging through the four seasons and carrying over a five-year or ten-year development, showing what can be expected in the future.

Your service can end with advice or, if the client wishes, you can go along and help select plants at nurseries and tools at stores. Actual planting should be done by the client himself.

The Cash Flow:

Your album of colored pictures may be an expense, although many gardeners already have scores of such pictures to choose from. The advertising budget is modest, since word of mouth will probably establish you. Your charges will probably be by the hour, $5 to $10. Another source of income is commission for the business you bring to the nursery and garden supply stores, if you make such arrangements with the proprietors.

SEASHELL AND DRIFTWOOD SHOP

The Idea:

One of the prettiest shops you can open is one devoted to seashells and driftwood. Driftwood is usually tinted in gray or bone color and shells are generally pink and white, or other pastel. Combine them and you achieve charisma.

If you like the idea of such a shop, open it in a room with lots of windows—has your house, by chance, an old-fashioned sun porch?—and arrange the shells and pieces of driftwood on shelves against the glass, interspersed with bright colored glass bottles and paperweights. Add some hanging baskets of ivy and people will come in, if only to admire.

They will probably buy, too. Driftwood is in demand to offset flower arrangements or just to use like bric-a-brac, and a surprisingly large section of the population make driftwood lamp bases, vases, wall sconces, mobiles, and jewelry. Beautiful or curious shells, too, appeal to almost everyone and there are quite a few shell collectors among the hobbyists.

Besides exhibiting the driftwood and shells in their natural state, you can work on them yourself. Seashell jewelry is popular and relatively easy to make. Crafting driftwood takes learning and special tools, manual and electric, but working in driftwood is widespread enough to make driftwood shows popular. For example, in 1971, the town of Grayland, Washington (population 550) drew an attendance of 4800 to its two-day driftwood show. If you can master this craft and display your items for sale, it will increase the drawing power of your shop. Classes might also be held, both in the making of shell jewelry and in the driftwood techniques.

Getting Started:

If you just want to offer pieces of driftwood and the single shells, all you need is a collection of each and a place to display them attractively. The beach is an excellent source of both shells and driftwood, although some beaches are pretty well stripped of the latter. Still, every tide and every storm may bring in a fresh supply. A walk in the woods, too, may lead to discovery of curiously shaped dead branches lying on the ground.

As for shells, besides those you can find yourself, the Yellow Pages, under "Shells-Marine," list wholesalers who will ship shells to dealers. Some of these are quite expensive, of course, if they are rare or very popular.

If you want to add objects made of shells and wood to your stock, and need instruction, then recourse to the public library will yield books on both crafts. Or perhaps you prefer to be associated with some friend who can be your craftsman and creator. The wholesaler will supply shells for jewelry at small cost. The tools for the driftwood work may be more expensive, unless your associate already has them.

The Cash Flow:

If you work this project from home, it is then free from rent. If you do rent, little space is required, although a good location, with plenty of shoppers passing by is important. Advertising is necessary, perhaps a continuing small ad with an artistic logo on the fashion pages. If there is a hobby publication in your vicinity, here is a good spot for an ad; also the programs of local plays, concerts, fashion shows, horse and dog shows.

Charges will vary with the beauty and rarity of the shells or wood pieces, but there should always be plenty of inexpensive shell earrings, bracelets, and necklaces for the teenage and young adult crowd.

BELTS ARE BACK

The Idea:

After years of ignoring the waistline, dress designers are marking the middle again. Belts are back and at higher prices than ever before.

There are all kinds of belts to be made, if you are interested—fabric, knitted and crocheted, leather, plastic, or macrame. All can be distinctive with ornamentation, buckles, embroidery, metal work, beads, even painting.

Getting Started:

To set up a successful belt studio, you need a flair for design, an eye for what will suit the individual customer or special dress, the digital facility to carry out the designs, and the right sort of promotion to make the studio known.

As to the exact methods of belt construction, if you have had a course in sewing, like that offered by Singer Sewing Machine branches or through the 4-H, the making of belts was included with instructions for dressmaking. Any sewing supply store sells belting, which can be covered and the buckle or other clasp added. Craft centers and the YWCA's or YWHA's often include leather work in their training courses. For learning macrame, consult your nearest needlework shop (needlework shops sometimes give lessons), craft center, or the public library for books of instructions.

A corner of your own house will do for a display room, with the belts hanging from racks or coiled in attractive boxes. If your window can be seen from the street, make a colorful eye catching sign to go against the glass. Design a striking sign for your lawn. Have cards printed with the name and address of your studio and the information that originally created belts, in regular stock or specially designed, are available. Leave these cards in mailboxes in affluent neighborhoods, and in beauty parlors, if the proprietors agree.

If you have a friend who has a dress shop or is a modiste, suggest that she might like to feature your belts, on consignment or commission.

The Cash Flow:

Not much outlay is required here. The materials are not expensive and can be picked up on remnant counters or in bargain centers. If you need to pay for a course of instruction, the cost will not be prohibitive.

Your charges should be low enough to give patrons the feeling that they have done well for themselves in getting a distinctive item at the same price that they would pay for a mass-produced belt in the stores. Keep an eye on the stocks of the stores, the prices and quality, and sell your belts accordingly. Add $5 to the price of a belt if you design and make it for a special outfit.

HATS

The Idea:

Nothing is more moribund during warm weather than the hat business. Males and females alike go hatless through the streets, even to church.

However, when the temperature drops below 32°, women, at least, generally put *something* on their heads—scarves, or knitted, fur or imitation fur caps. This "something" might as well be pretty and becoming.

If you are good at knitting and crocheting, at designing and copying, and at sewing together pieces of fabric and fur into distinctive creations, then why not open for business in this line? Instructions often come along with purchases of knitting and crocheting materials. Former experience in a hat shop or millinery department would give you valuable techniques, but more important is flair for design and an instinct for the right style for the customer.

Getting Started:

Run a small ad in a newspaper or church or club publication describing your assortment of styles, expressed in vibrant prints and colors and a variety of fabrics, some of them water repellent. Have cards printed with your name and address and the service offered and put them in mailboxes and on bulletin boards. Hand letter a sign to go on your front lawn, or have one painted. Tell a feature writer about your venture, a bold one in these hatless days, and suggest pictures for the paper of your prettiest headwear on your prettiest customers.

The Cash Flow:

Expenses: advertising, publicity, and cost of materials. The latter can be picked up at remnant sales, on bargain counters, and at bazaars.

In enterprises of this type, there is usually one charge for a regular design, another for a design created for the individual. The first of these might be $5 to $10; the second, $12 to $20.

SMALL PAINTINGS

The Idea:

An Artists' Street Mart, modeled on New York's Greenwich Village exhibit, is found in more and more towns and cities. All kinds of art is there: noveau, primitive, impressionistic, expressionistic, you name it.

Forgetting about art appreciation and taking the purely commercial point of view, the observer will probably note that the small, inexpensive pieces move, while the big, costlier ones are slow sellers. Most people come just to look around but would like to take *something* away, and the little pictures not only cost less but are more portable, and easier to place in homes or offices.

A New York woman capitalizes on this. All year she paints little pictures, tiny landscapes, ships, birds, flowers, faces, abstract designs in miniature, anything. She buys small frames when she sees a bargain. The painting and framing, of course, can be done at home and with a minimum of space and equipment. Her only expense is painting material and frames.

Getting Started:

If you are interested in doing likewise, here is an activity that can open an exciting, creative way to supplement your income. If an outdoor art show or fair is already in your town or city, then you need only find out its dates, how to secure a good display spot, and turn up with your wares. If your city does not have such an event, perhaps you might try to organize one, through local art schools, painting clubs, and the Chamber of Commerce.

The Cash Flow:

The New York woman described above charges between $2 and $5 each for her paintings. The profit, of course, is governed by how many she has been able to paint during the year. She invariably sells all these little pictures, so modestly priced and so easy to carry away.

WINDOW TRIMMING

The Idea:

Major stores have their own window trimming staff, but smaller businesses can't afford this. So here is an opportunity for the free-lancer.

What makes a free-lance window trimmer? Primarily, she should have the imagination to adapt her talents equally well to the window of a glamorous imported clothing store and that of an electrical appliance store, to turn from deluxe gourmet foods to plumbing supplies.

To be a good window trimmer, you need the ability to take two elements—limited space and few, or many, props— and combine them in such a way that they *say* something. Such an ability is inborn to a degree but can be developed and sharpened by observation, adaptation of the work of others, and experience. Study the windows in the big department stores in your own town and in any city you visit, and see how they build around a theme or idea—seasonal cheer, opening of school, or the approach of some local event, like a theatre performance of season, the local fair, horse or dog show. Study color effects and lighting. Theoretically, you should not crowd a window, but sometimes the store owner wants many items displayed and it is up to you to carry out this wish as effectively as possible.

Getting Started:

You can do your own promotion and running of the business from home. Direct mail might be your best medium. Send short, comprehensive letters offering your services to as many stores as you think can use them, followed up with telephone calls and requests for interviews. For the interview, if you have photographs of window displays you have done, by all means take them along. If you suggest a trial demonstration, this will give you the opportunity to show your prospective client what you can do. All this involves little expense. The materials you need for your work—merchandise items, dummies, decorative paper, strings of electric lights, artificial flowers and foliage, stuffed fish, artificial snow—are provided by your clients.

The Cash Flow:

Charges should vary by the size and number of the windows. For a small shop, with only one window, you perhaps charge for a single job of decoration. If the owner wants to contract for several months or a year, with weekly changes of decoration, the charge might be $100 to $200 a month. For a store with two or more big windows, the charges might be 50% higher.

CUSTOM-MADE SLIP COVERS AND DRAPERIES

The Idea:

Can you make slip covers and draperies for your own home that have a genuinely custom-made look? If you can, if you have real expertise in this work, along with a sense of color and design, why not earn an income through this skill?

Getting Started:

You should have a good chance of prospering in this activity. People move a lot in these restless days; get tired of their old decor; mothers want to refurbish the house after their children have passed the drop-bread-and-jam-on-the-davenport stage. Then there are the new real estate developments. If you live near one or more of these, the families that move into the new houses probably will clamor for your services.

Of course you will have to make these services known. One neighbor tells another about you, and this is good. In fact, it may be the best way for people to learn of your project because, while it is an excellent means of publicity, it is slow enough so that you will not receive too many orders at once. That is a trap you should avoid. If you accept more orders than you can fill with a reasonable promptness, the good will of your business, that precious intangible, will suffer.

If you have made your own draperies and slip covers, you already have the necessary equipment—a big cutting table and a sewing machine sturdy enough to handle heavy fabrics.

Your customers will probably consult you on which designs and fabrics to choose and, after a viewing of their homes and the rooms to be decorated, you can offer good advice. On the visit, you can take measurements from which to make muslin patterns for the slip covers, returning for a fitting before cutting into the chosen fabric. Draperies, of course, are made direct from measurements, so each window must be carefully measured.

You may want to supply the fabrics yourself, and if so you need a sample case for the swatches. Fabric manufacturers generally will supply such a sample case gratis.

The Cash Flow:

If you already have your sewing machine and cutting table, you need not make this initial investment. Working from home, and with little or no advertising, you have a low overhead. You are, therefore, able to undersell the decorating houses, a big factor in getting customers.

CUSTOM FRAMING

The Idea:

A part-time job that has grown into full-time for a good many of its practitioners is custom framing, that is, providing a special frame for a picture that sets off its individual appeal.

A well designed, well chosen frame adds greatly to the effect of a painting, print, etching, photograph, or to a piece of fine needlework, a diploma or citation. Perhaps, when you have seen an eye-catching print on the wall of a friend's house, and have learned that the frame cost a good deal more than the print, you wondered why. But when you see a copy of the print, unframed, and contrast it with the framed print, its colors brought out, its form emphasized, and the whole effect blending into and focusing the decorative scheme of the room, you begin to understand.

More and more people nowadays realize the value of a custom frame over the run-of-the-mill job, and they are willing to pay for the difference.

If you can turn out custom frames, your sources of business can include individual artists who need the best possible display of their work; museums and art galleries; schools and colleges wanting to frame documents and scrolls, as well as portraits and other pictures; photographers; retail stores with art departments or needing frames for posters, notices, and window display items; and interior decorators who often design a whole room around a strikingly framed picture.

This is, of course, a highly skilled craft, but one that can be learned, with application and the right instruction. The custom framer must know mouldings, when to use hardwood, softwood, or composition, whether to finish with paint, stain, lacquer, how to cut, miter, join, blend, repair; must know the different methods of mounting, with and without mats, when to use stretchers; must be a good worker with mats, whether of board of cloth, laminated or textured, with liners and glass cutting processes. One successful custom framer says that an important secret of his work is in the squaring off of the corners of a frame and the concealment of joints. An inexpensive commercial frame often gaps at the corners where the frame is joined. This man fills in any hairline joints in his frames, then touches it up with paint if needed, and uses

expensive moulding which he contours at the joint so there is
no obvious break in pattern. Where store-bought frames may
use one nail at right angles to the frame to hold the corner,
this framer uses epoxy glue. By such special painstaking
details is custom framing distinguished.

Getting Started:

How do you learn all this? Craft centers may offer courses
and some YWCA's include this instruction in their curricula.
There is a correspondence course entitled "FrameCrafters,"
based in Orange, California, which advertises in magazines
and Sunday supplements.

When you are skilled enough to start professionally, you
can work out of your home or, more ambitiously, operate a
store, or even, eventually, a wholesale-retail business.

The Cash Flow:

The mark-up is high. A Florida firm charges $40 to $300
for a frame. They sell both wholesale and retail, figuring a
20% wholesale mark-up. Expenses vary, depending on
whether you have rent and on the extent of your advertising.
Perhaps the best way to get your first clients is to make
personal calls on prospects and show them some of your work.

PHOTOGRAPHER

The Idea:

Camera buffs are a dime a dozen, but once in a while
there is one who can catch the essence of a storm scene, a
gracious interior, a dilapidated tenement, a deserted farm, a
laughing baby, a frolicking kitten, an individual face. It's
more than just getting the image on the film, unblurred. The
"feel" of the person or episode must be there.

If you have this gift, even if only in a relatively slight
degree, you can have a profitable sideline, perhaps even a full-

time job. People will pay for worthy commemoration of special things in their lives: weddings, parties, children, home before it is sold or torn down, the party the office gives to a retiree. And we all believe we owe a portrait of ourselves to posterity.

Getting Started:

At the start, your studio can be within your home, although if business grows it will soon call for quarters of its own. The new location should be where prospective clients will pass by and see window displays, yet rent should not eat up profits, a combination that will necessitate considerable research into neighborhoods, real estate offices, and the advertising columns of newspapers.

Adequate equipment is important from the inception of the enterprise. As a photographer ready to become professional, you know what you need. Second hand equipment is sometimes the answer at first.

The Cash Flow:

As long as you work at home, you have no rent and you should be sure the business justifies it before you add this expense. Advertisements are always useful but word spread by enthusiastic subjects of your art will bring the best results. Watch the newspapers, especially the social items, for weddings coming up, the date of charity balls, and so on. A wide acquaintance would be a big help to you, since you will hear of who is graduating, who is planning an elaborate party, a christening, a special luncheon.

If you do run ads, the local newspapers should never be neglected, and another good spot is the program of a local event, theatrical, musical, or sport.

Your charges for portraits, events like weddings, conventions, vary according to the time and film involved. Then there are special assignments, like following a prominent person around and taking candid shots.

Have you a specialty, or do you want to cover all these phases?

MAKING PAPER FLOWERS

The Idea:

If you have exceptionally nimble fingers and an equally exceptional eye for color and design, you might corner the paper flower market in your vicinity.

This is not as bizarre as it sounds. A woman in a southern city found herself house-bound while her children were small. One day at Christmas time she began to amuse herself by making poinsettas and leaves out of red and green paper. The result was so good that a commercially minded friend persuaded her that she might have the beginning of a money-making project.

Getting Started:

She did. She followed a course which might appeal to you, too, if this activity sounds like one suited to you. She made more and more different kinds of flowers, mostly of the fantastic type not too closely following nature but gorgeous and imaginative. She found, however, that, while she likes to design and cut out the petals and leaves, and wire, glue, and combine them, she does not like to sell and has no gift in that direction. So the commercially minded neighbor was called in and offered a share in the business if she would contact possible buyers and arrange terms. This arrangement has worked well for both women.

The Cash Flow:

The flowers are sold wholesale, singly, and in baskets, to boutiques, gift shops, and department stores. The women now have orders to fill for banquets, conventions, hotel lobbies, and doctors' and dentists' waiting rooms. The seller goes out in person, a basket of blooms on arm. The business does not advertise; word of mouth publicity has been sufficient. The very inexpensive materials required are colored tissue paper, green florist tape, a clear lacquer spray, scissors, and wire.

ADVERTISING AGENCY

The Idea:

The United States Census Bureau (1972) lists 68 advertising agencies, with paid employees, owned by women, along with 1,827 ad agencies owned by women with no employees, in other words, one-woman set-ups.

Those experienced in this field take some exception to the "one-woman" inference. The consensus is that the "one woman" may be the sole proprietor or corporate owner of her agency, but she needs a lot of free lance help to run this complicated business. This is not an activity that one likes the sound of, rents an office for, and enters into. Experience and background are musts.

Getting Started:

Before you go out on your own here, you need several years apprenticeship with a recognized ad agency, as copy writer or artist, worker in lay-out, typography, photography. You can be good in any or none of these and still start your own agency, hiring free lance workers to take care of whatever is outside your scope. But one thing you must do for yourself: sell your services as an account executive and plan a successful ad campaign. That means expert knowledge of budgeting, media, timing, a flair for forecasting, and ability to analyze results. This compendium of expertise is not acquired quickly, only through time and the hard school of experience.

You need contacts, not only with possible clients but with

those who will give the best service in art, lay-out, and typography, copy writing, the men and women who will supply the skills you lack. You need to keep up with the ever-changing picture of marketing in general and of your product or products in particular. Do new laws affect them? Which type of media reaches the consumer who is most likely to respond to your message?

The Cash Flow:

You do not need large office space but a "good" address is important, one in a building of at least fair prestige and also located in a spot accessible to clients and your free lancers. Your own media advertising can be confined to the Yellow Pages, but your rent, telephone, and postage bills will probably be considerable not to mention what you pay the free lancers.

Besides all this, you need a resilient temperament, one that will not be overcast with gloom when a client, for whom you have done what you think is a superb job, inexplicably takes his account elsewhere. C'est la vie in the ad agency business.

Still, according to our country's census, more than 1,800 women are in this field, going it alone or with the help of an average of five employees. By the 1972 figures, they grossed $8,606,000. The 68 with employees averaged $127,000 in gross receipts. These are 1972 figures. Present day grosses may supposedly be considerably higher.

7.

HANDICRAFTS—
GOING STRONG ON
THE CURRENT SCENE

WEAVING

The Idea:

The ancient craft of weaving has quite a place on the contemporary scene. Weavers are encountered coast to coast. An indication of the extent of general interest is the presence in most of our major cities of shops devoted entirely to looms and weaving equipment. Suits, skirts, placemats, draperies, counterpanes, and other items of handwoven fabrics can bring good prices, sold retail on your own or wholesale to craft shops. However, an experienced weaver, asked for advice to those who wish to enter this field, maintains that, unless you have a real flair for salesmanship, the only way to secure a good financial return is through teaching classes in weaving. These may be either private, if good studio space is available to you, or in one of the many colleges and other institutions offering weaving courses. Another field for weavers is weaving therapy used in many hospitals. This, of course, is done under the direction of trained therapists and doctors.

Getting Started:

First, of course, you need to study. This can be done in some universities and colleges, especially in the Adult Education divisions, or in craft centers offering such training. Some YWCA's have weaving courses. Another way is to study with an individual weaver to learn at least the basics and then go on alone, with the help of some of the excellent books available on weaving techniques. You must acquire your own loom or looms, as well as other equipment.

If you wish to teach in a university or college, it is advisable to have won some awards and citations at craft shows. These shows are announced in the trade publications, including *Craft Horizons,* published by America House, and *Handweaver and Craftsman*, New York. Both may probably be found in your public library.

A weaver can publicize herself through small mail ads in the right newspapers and in church, temple, and club magazines. A free lecture before a club or school often brings pupils. Weaving, with its traditions of the past and its adaptation to modern living, usually interests local feature writers and a good story, with photographs, helps a lot. Reprints of the story should be ordered and enclosed in promotion letters.

The Cash Flow:

It is fairly expensive to set up as a weaver. The courses of study vary in price with the different institutions and teachers but are seldom excessive. Your looms will probably come to $200 or $300 for the smaller sizes and $600 or $700 for the larger, plus the price of shuttles, spool reels, bobbin winders, and such equipment. Add to these initial expenses the continuing expense of whatever advertising you do. You need studio space. If this is available at home, that is best. If not, you will have to rent, if you teach on your own.

Perhaps you can calculate your price per student based

on a class of six, to bring you a return of $60 to $100 a pupil for a course of ten lessons.

CREWEL WORK

The Idea:

Crewel work, that intricate embroidery of days gone by, has made a big comeback in the '60's and '70's. Crewel work pillows, upholstery for wing chairs, counterpanes, curtains, covers for foot stools, bring high prices, although the time involved cuts down profits.

The real money is in crewel work classes. You can start a class, perhaps at a summer resort where people have lots of time. You may be surprised that the presence of men in such a class is less and less of a rarity.

If you like teaching and continuing the activity throughout the year, you may build up a following and have a waiting list of pupils. If you are a writer, you can write books of instruction. Publishers are receptive to books on arts and crafts, due to their current popularity. If you are not a writer yourself, perhaps you can collaborate with a writing friend. You will probably have the opportunity to lecture and demonstrate your work at libraries and museums, and possibly, like Erica Wilson, be featured on television.

Getting Started:

First, naturally, you must work up an impressive degree of expertise. Your first professional work might be to fill orders for individuals and small specialty shops. Then on to teaching, which provides the means for significant advancement. This sort of instruction is better given in the informal atmosphere of your own home, although as time goes on you will probably be asked to hold courses at craft centers. As for advertising, put small, continuing ads, with a distinctive logo, on the family pages and in the hobby columns of newspapers.

Make a study of the publications read by the clientele you wish to attract and take small ads.

The Cash Flow:

A suggested scale of charges would be $12 for four two-hour lessons, ten in a class. This means $120 a course, or a return to you of $15 per teaching hour. Depending on the number of pupils, you can have two or three courses scheduled each week.

Another source of income would be to buy wools and designs wholesale and sell them to your pupils. Still another is to hold a show every six months of your own and your students' work, all items for sale. On your students' sales you receive 15%.

HAND-EMBROIDERED SWEATERS

The Idea:

A plain sweater can be turned into a glamorous cocktail or evening garment when it is embroidered with sparkling beads, spangles, metallic threads, shining satin, or crewel. A woman clever at this sort of work can set up a profitable small business by effecting such transformations.

Getting Started:

If you are already expert at this kind of embroidery, you can start right in. If you need coaching, shop around and find someone who can give your skill the finishing touches and take lessons. Your teacher might be a woman who works, or has worked for a fine embroidery house. Such firms can be found in the Yellow Pages and you will have to take it from there in running down the right instructor.

While you are convincing yourself that you are ready to set up as a professional, glamorize your own sweaters and some for your family and friends. When you know you are prepared, insert a tempting ad in the newspaper you think most likely to reach prospective customers, like "HAND-EMBROIDERED SWEATERS. Give Your Plain Sweaters The Paris Look, The Luxury Touch." Have some cards printed, with your name, address, and telephone number, and "Hand-Embroidered Sweaters" in the lower left hand corner. Leave these cards in mail boxes and ask establishments such as beauty parlors to let you keep a supply at their appointment desks. Your satisfied customers will tell their friends about you and probably this will be the most effective publicity of all.

When a sweater is finished, it should be mailed, delivered, or picked up in an attractive box, with your name and address and the legend "Hand-Embroidered Sweaters" conspicuously showing. Don't forget to design a distinctive label to sew inside each sweater.

The Cash Flow:

You work at home. Newspaper advertising and the printed cards are not expensive. Add to this the cost of boxes with your name and imprint and of the special labels, as well as for the embroidery materials.

As for charges, this is skilled, exacting work. You are justified in charging $10 to $15 an hour for the time spent on an individual sweater.

DECOUPAGE

The Idea:

Decoupage, an 18th Century craft revived with enthusiasm in the 20th, may be defined as the art of decorating surfaces permanently with cutouts. Almost any object, from a tiny pillbox to a tall secretary-desk, can be embellished by the accomplished decoupeur. Decoration can be in traditional or contemporary style, today's decoupeurs work in both.

Decoupage is for the perfectionist. You must have the patience and precision to carry out an intricate operation, but in the end, if you are gifted, you have an exquisite box, lamp, or tray, or a magnificent and valuable piece of furniture.

Getting Started:

The beginner needs step-by-step instruction in choice of object (start with something simple), covering, the use of paints, colored pencils, crayon or gold leaf, the correct method of cutting figures from prints, how to create a design and how to cover the design finally with varnish or lacquer and rub it to a soft glow. In some localities, decoupeurs gather regularly in "clinics," meetings where they compare notes on progress and help each other. Experts in decoupage often teach and are to be found in almost every town or city of any size. Instruction is also given at some craft centers and YWCA's. When you visit museums, ask if they have examples of decoupage made in the 1700's. Some museums have such exhibits. There are fine books of instruction on decoupage, if you have the patience to go it alone.

If you have the natural talent and develop it to a high degree, you will probably find a market for your creations. Handsome lamps, paperweights, trays of all sizes, switchplates, boxes of all sizes and shapes, hand mirrors, and many other pieces can sell well. Orders can be taken to decorate furniture.

When your reputation has grown sufficiently, you will perhaps take pupils, singly or in class. Well known decoupeurs sometimes teach in several cities, going from one art center to the other on regular days, or giving special courses. If you are a good lecturer and have outstanding pieces to exhibit, clubs may invite you to speak.

The Cash Flow:

The financial return is risky. To learn decoupage does not involve a great deal of expense, especially if you practice a lot at home. However, to develop expertise often does take time and patience. How much you charge for your pieces depends a great deal on the growth of your reputation as a decoupeur. Individual orders can be taken, and you can try to place some of your wares in fine gift shops and on the appropriate counters of department stores. Considering the time involved, you should get a good price—if you can. Decoupage lamps in stores sometimes sell for $50 and considerably more, and wooden, lidded boxes with handles, made into purses and decoupaged, have sold as high as $75 each. These, however, are ideal prices. In whatever you charge, you must consider the cost of materials, including paint, varnish, brushes, cleaning fluid, etc., not to mention the bases and other parts for the lamps. The price for lectures and lessons depends much on your locality and the income bracket of your clients.

WRAPPING GIFT PACKAGES

The Idea:

A pleasant and seasonably active small service business can be organized if you are skilled in the wrapping of gift packages. There are plenty of people, especially men, who buy nice presents for family and friends, for their office force or other business associates, and who are all thumbs when it comes to wrapping them. True, big stores will gift wrap purchases, but this is usually a mass production, following set patterns. Small shops, which often have the best selection of individual and "different" gifts, seldom do any striking gift wrapping. You will offer an artistic, fanciful, or plain, beautiful, and dignified wrapping.

So, if you are talented in this direction—can make a package glamorous and sparkling for Christmas . . . so lovely with pastel paper and ribbon that the woman whose birthday it is hates to disturb its beauty to open it . . . amusing with funny stickers for a child's gift . . . plain but rich looking for a man . . . designed ad infinitem to fit the personality of the recipient—then you probably are already in demand to wrap for your family, friends, and business acquaintances. Why not get paid for it?

Getting Started:

Before you begin, it would be a good idea to work at Christmas time at the wrapping counter of a department store. You learn about the amount of paper necessary for a certain number of average-sized packages, to check the scotch tape and ribbon supply. The designs may give you inspiration for adaptations in your own work.

The libraries do not offer much literature for study on gift wrapping. Your public library may have a copy of H. Oka's book, "How To Wrap Five Eggs," which deals with gift wrapping in the Japanese manner. It might be well to add the Japanese to your styles of wrapping. The more variety you can offer, the better.

The Cash Flow:

You can do this work at home, perhaps devoting a corner of a room to shelves made glamorous by your bright rolls of paper in solid colors and printed designs, by the sheen of ribbon, and perhaps a poster showing a delectably wrapped package. If you can make such a poster yourself, well and good. If not, a friend who has studied art may be persuaded to make it for you.

Expenses? No rent. Just the price of paper and other materials, good scissors, and paper cutters. You will have to learn to buy the paper in the proper amounts and only experience will teach you this know-how. You might find it useful to run small ads in the local papers and neighborhood publications, especially at Christmas and Easter and as Mother's Day approaches. Ads in house organs of large businesses located near you might bring business.

Your charges should be high, say $1 for a small package, $2 for average size, and $3 and up for a large one, with special prices for a dozen or more assorted sized packages. This is not big business, but it is a good way to supplement a family income. And if you live in a large city, publicize adequately, and provide brilliantly designed packages, you *might* grow and even have to have associates to handle the volume of orders.

DOLLS

The Idea:

If you are a doll fancier, you can find an interesting career in collecting, repairing, dressing, and displaying these small replicas of the human race. Dolls are perhaps the oldest toy and predate written history by many centuries. Museums that have doll houses on exhibition can count on interested crowds made up of men and women, as well as children. People collect antique dolls, those survivors of the past that often give actual evidence of the dress, coiffures, and tastes of bygone days. These antique dolls, inherited or purchased, are often in bad condition, and the owners will pay well for an expert repair job. Sometimes the garments of the doll are in tatters and she needs to be clothed again in dress of her period. A New England woman specializes in such work, replacing arms, legs, hair, and eyes and, if necessary, redressing the dolls, making the clothes of old velvet, lace, and silk she finds in thrift shops. Another woman specializes in copying antique dolls from china head to fabric arms and legs. She dresses them in appropriate costume, farthingale, Empire style, hoop skirt, bustle, or what have you. Still another woman is a costumer for dolls and recently won a prize for her eighteen-inch Queen Elizabeth I, in wide pink satin skirts and beaded bodice. A fourth woman dresses modern dolls in contemporary wardrobes, making trousseaus, resort wear, and single dresses.

Getting Started:

If you feel like following in the footsteps of any of the above women, dollwise, the last described would be the easiest. You need to have knowledge of dressmaking, plus imagination. For the others, you need special training. There are courses on doll repair and doll making and they can be located through museums and historical societies. There is a real doll cult, made up of fanciers all over the world, and many handsome books have been published on doll lore.

Cultivate as wide an acquaintance as possible in the arts and crafts world, the antique collectors, the historical-minded. You will encounter many who pick up dolls for themselves and others. Advertise in the publications these people read, the hobby magazines, and the like. Set up a display of your best dolls to catch interest. When you are well started, try to get the local television station to send a reporter to look at your work.

The Cash Flow:

This is no way to make a fortune, but the costs are not high. Your course of study, if you take one, is the initial expense, advertising and purchase of materials, the continuing. You can probably work from home. If you must work elsewhere, perhaps you can join with some other women at a craft center.

Charges for repairing or copying or costuming antique dolls should be high, perhaps $10 an hour. If you make a wardrobe for a modern doll, perhaps $7 or $8 an hour.

REUPHOLSTERING

The Idea:

To be a reupholsterer good enough to charge for work

done takes a real pro. This is a tough trade and unless you are skilled, earnest, and dedicated to hard work, better forget it. But if you have learned on your own furniture and that of family and friends, and if the results can meet comparison with those of department stores and drapery shop upholsterers, then you can open up for business. You should not lack customers. It is usually not only less expensive but more convenient for a householder to have a piece reupholstered than to buy a new one. The one already in place probably suits the room in size and shape and the family is used to it. Besides reupholstering furniture for your clientele, you can canvass the auctions and estate sales and pick up old wing chairs, sofas, and so on, take them home and transform them and make a considerable profit on a resale.

Getting Started:

If you have not already had a course in this work at a trade school, adult education, or craft center, or possibly by correspondence, better take such a course, even if you consider yourself already good.

You need work space, in basement or garage, and the tools of your trade are many and necessary, including factory-type sewing machine, button covering machine, padded work benches, special hammer, shears, webbing stretcher, ripper, skewer, straight and curved needles, stuffing regulator, springs, fillers, welt cording, tacks, screws, dowels. Unless you require the customer to supply the fabric, you need a sample display.

One problem is the cartage from the customer's home to your place and back. Here is where you need male help, from the owner of a pick-up truck or perhaps some member of your own family. You can, of course, specify that customers do their own delivery and pick-up, but this not only lessens good will but necessitates your lowering prices to meet competition which does deliver.

Advertise in the local paper and Yellow Pages. Printed cards put in mail boxes may produce new customers. Word of mouth will probably prove your most effective publicity.

The Cash Flow:

It will take at least several hundred dollars to start, what with the cost of the sewing machine and equipment. Your advertising budget need not be large, but should represent a continuing expense.

You will probably be wise to undersell the upholsterers shops and the department stores in your neighborhood. This will bring you orders, especially in the beginning. Of course, you do not want too many orders—it is bad business to take more than you can fill in a reasonable time. Perhaps you should calculate your work by the hour. This ranges from $12 to $20 an hour depending on the difficulty of the work, locality, and competition.

CHAIR CANING

The Idea:

Re-caning antique and heirloom chairs, or any chair needing caning, for that matter, is a craft that you master with relative ease, provided you have reasonably deft fingers and the patience to learn from one of those caning kits that can be ordered by mail. You often see ads for such kits, along with a booklet of instructions, in magazine columns and in Sunday supplements. Craft centers and adult education institutes also sometimes give courses in chair caning.

Getting Started:

Your workshop might be a room in your house, a part of your basement or garage, an attic, an unused shed or, if none of these are available, rented space. If you rent, it need not be in a high priced part of town. If no rent at home or low rent elsewhere can help keep your prices lower than your competitors', people will gladly drive their station wagons to your obscure location. You do not even need to plan on parking accommodations, since chairs to be re-caned are generally light enough in weight to be carried out to a double-parked vehicle. Just be sure any rented quarters are weathertight, since a leaking roof or a badly fitted window might let rain in on your customers' chairs.

The Cash Flow:

Expenses are not great, especially if you can work at home. You need the right tools and a supply of natural cane and raffia. Your instructor is sometimes a supplier, too, or can guide you to a good place to obtain your needed items.

A small ad running at regular intervals in the local newspaper is almost a must in getting customers and adding new ones as time goes on. The original customers will probably be repeaters and will recommend you to their friends, but word of mouth publicity perhaps needs a little supplementing.

An attractive, easily read sign announcing your services is another must, even if you have to pay well for having it designed and painted.

Since you will be caring for other people's property while you work the chairs into your schedule, be sure to check with your insurance man as to adequate protection.

Charges for chair caning vary. In a major city, a price for re-caning a ladderback antique chair was quoted at $40. The same chair was taken to a shop in the suburbs and re-caned for $15.

HOBBY SCHOOL

The Idea:

If you are both skillful and versatile in handicrafts and

needlework, and good at games like checkers, scrabble, and monopoly, you may be able to cash in on teaching members of the new leisure class, that is, people with shorter work hours, housewives who have systemized their work and whose children are in school or grown, retirees, even people on vacation or waiting for a new job to open up. You can let it be known that you teach arts and crafts and gamesmanship, and also sell the equipment necessary, such as that for leather-work, candlemaking, knitting, oil or water color painting, needlepoint, or the games.

Getting Started:

Can you hold your hobby school at home? You need space and light. Your basement might provide the space but how about the light? An attic is not so good because your older students might find stairs hard to climb and sometimes attics are not heated. However, if you can adapt part of your home to this purpose, so much the better. If not, you will have to seek out a suitable place to rent.

Next, you need the materials required for instruction, plus work and game tables and chairs. The room should be cheerful, with perhaps bright posters on the walls, light paint, and colorful linoleum on the floor.

The equipment for sale should be attractively arranged on shelves along the wall.

If you are starting this project, tell everyone you know and urge them to tell all their friends. Write, type, or print notices for the bulletin boards of senior citizen clubs and other community centers. Have the ad man of your local newspaper help you design a small, distinctive ad to run regularly in his columns. Ask the newspaper if they would be interested in sending a reporter to get a story, with pictures, of your project.

The Cash Flow:

You will probably quote the price of instruction in

courses, not single lessons. If you think it would take 20 class lessons of an hour each to teach a student some skill in a craft like candlemaking, then calculate your time at $10 per student per hour, or whatever price you decide on.

NEEDLEPOINT SHOP

The Idea:

The great needlepoint boom started some years ago and shows no sign of abating. Not only women, but men—Henry Fonda, for one—find in this ancient skill an artistic medium and a regulator for nerves much more healthy than cigarette smoking.

Getting Started:

Want to capitalize on this public fondness for creativity in wool and canvas? First, if you think you need to increase your own expertise, courses are offered by stores, some YWCA's, and craft centers. You might begin to go pro by accepting orders for rugs, pillowcases, purses, eyeglass cases, and so on, done in needlepoint, and taking a few pupils.

Then, if your own and the community's interest in your work grows, perhaps you will open a small shop. Before you do this, you will have to decide whether you have enough capital of your own or if you need to borrow from the bank (see Chapter II), and you must look for a suitable location (see Chapter III). You need to be accessible to shoppers, which means a "good" neighborhood, but you require only small space, which means you need pay rent on a limited area. You could even take over part of a dress shop and share expenses.

In your own quarters, you can sell your original designs, as well as thread, wool, canvas, and needles, and hold your own classes of instruction.

Promotion through word of mouth will probably be your

number one publicity, but you should get permission to put up signs in neighboring stores, in senior citizen centers, and retirement colonies. Women's club and hobby club contacts are invaluable.

The Cash Flow:

Based on an average 30% profit for supplies and a 50% mark-up for custom work, you can achieve a good return for your efforts in a business that also brings interesting contacts with all sorts of people.

8.

FOOD—FASCINATING, VITAL, PROFITABLE

CATERING FROM HOME

The Idea:

A catering business can be operated from a home kitchen. When you think of it, there are many occasions and places where competent catering is needed and welcome: business luncheons and banquets, fund-raising dinners of charity groups, luncheon clubs, political meetings, weddings, engagement parties, bridge tournaments, cocktail parties, dances. The list can go on and on, and perhaps might include regular daily lunches for private schools, if there are any in your locality.

Needed is someone (like you) at the head of the project, who is a more-than-good cook; who can plan menus to suit the occasion; can market economically and still ensure quality; can supply the proper equipment, i.e., table silver, china (or plastic dishes), glasses (unbreakable), and coffee urns; and who delivers in the family station wagon, at least at first, perhaps later acquiring a light delivery truck.

Getting Started:

Customers may initially be obtained by word of mouth, later through telephone campaigns, direct mail, and ads in local newspapers and on radio. The news will get around after you have had some successes in providing appetizing food, delivered on time and served with grace and efficiency. Incidentally, if you do include serving in your contract, you will need assistance. Perhaps members of your family can be pressed into helping if you present the work to them not only as a challenge, but as paid-for fun.

The Cash Flow:

Expenses do not include rent, since you operate from home. Gasoline for your station wagon should be counted in. Your advertising budget, comprising small newspaper ads, direct mail, and telephone, can be developed as the business grows. The mark-up of profit should be 50%—that is, a dish that costs $1.00 should be sold for $1.50; a luncheon that costs you $200, should be billed $300 to the organization ordering it.

COOKING CLASSES

The Idea:

Now-a-days almost anyone who can read can be a passable cook, since good books of instruction abound, with easy-to-follow recipes. Still, it is more fun to learn the basics or to extend culinary knowledge in a group. If you have made of cooking both a hobby and an art, as differentiated from a daily drudgery, then perhaps you would be good at imparting your specialized skills to others by teaching classes. Both you and your pupils can enjoy the sessions. Cooking is like any other craft, it can be learned by trial and error, but it is easier to take advantage of what others have learned through the ages.

Getting Started:

Convince people, through your ads and promotional letters and interviews, that brides are not the only people interested in being good cooks. Women who have hated cooking for years would *like* to like it, since they have to do it anyway. And lots of men live alone and can no longer afford to eat in restaurants every day. Men make good cooks. The traditional figure in a chef's cap is masculine. Get enough men in your classes and it will probably be easy to interest a reporter from the local newspaper to come in and take pictures and write a story about you and your students. If this story is a good presentation, have multigraphed copies made and enclose them in letters to prospective pupils.

Equipment and location may be problems, unless you live in a fairly accessible spot and have not only a large, but an oversized kitchen, with plenty of cupboard space for the right pots and pans. Ideally, you should have the latest in electric range and oven. However, you can adapt to what conditions you have. If your kitchen is not large, have smaller classes, given more frequently. One class might meet Mondays and Thursdays, another Tuesdays and Fridays. Pupils who are housewives will probably prefer morning sessions, say, 9:30 to 11:00. Business people will have to come in the evenings, or perhaps for a longer session on Saturdays. If your equipment lacks some fancy modern touches, then fit your curriculum to your limitations and, as you prosper, you may want to reinvest your profits in the latest appliances and gadgets.

The Cash Flow:

This is a project operated from home, so eliminate rent from your expenses. If you can raise five or six pupils to begin with, they may sing your praises and bring in more aspiring gourmet cooks. A small ad on what used to be called the Woman's Page in the local paper might attract attention in the right quarters. Also, if your budget rises to it, you might take a few seconds of advertising on the local radio station, or even share with a group of other advertisers in sponsoring some program on local television. Cultivate women's clubs and community organizations. They bring contacts.

Your charges should be for a course of five to ten lessons, perhaps $50 for five, $90 for ten.

SANDWICH SUPPLIER

The Idea:

If you are good at watching the Food Pages in your daily paper and taking advantage of price breaks on ham, cheese, eggs, canned sardines, and so on, and if you can make a deal with a baker to buy bread in quantity, then think of a mass sandwich business. Perhaps your best clients would be bar and beer taverns that do not serve food, but whose customers sometimes get hungry between drinks. Also, you might get orders from offices, if you can undersell the lunch places. You would probably set up a schedule of receiving orders and buying supplies the day before you make up the sandwiches; then prepare the sandwiches in the morning, wrap them individually, and deliver then. If you don't have a car, this might pose a problem.

For the customers you get this way you probably do not have to chase down fancy recipes. The old tried and true ham, cheese, and such fillings will no doubt be preferred, which makes it easier to plan and shop.

Getting Started:

To begin, you might make up a couple of dozen sandwiches, carefully wrapped, and take them around to places where you think orders can be secured. If you get a bar on one side of the street and word gets to his competitor on the other side, the latter will probably give you an order, too. Canvass the big office buildings. If the elevator starter won't let you go up to solicit orders, retire gracefully, get a list of businesses in the building, and send them a short sales letter, describing your service and quoting prices. If your sandwiches are already ordered, you are on a different footing with the starter and he will let you go up.

The Cash Flow:

You will have to do some figuring, taking the price of the bread and fillers, plus your gasoline for delivery, and calculate the price of the single sandwich. Give yourself 100% mark-up, slightly less for the bars, which will order by the dozen. The only other expense is the stationery and postage for your direct mailings.

FAMILY RECIPE

The Idea:

Is there a recipe—ethnic, regional, or just characteristic of your family—that your grandmother or great aunt passed on to you for cake, jelly, soup, smoked meat, or what not? If so, and if it really is as good as your forebears thought it, perhaps here is a product for which you can find a specialized gourmet market. Even if the original recipe needs a little adjusting, a skilled and creative cook can adapt it to modern tastes, while keeping the glamour of tradition. (My ancestor served these brandied peaches in a dinner for Lafayette. My grandmother brought this cake recipe from Vienna. Etc., etc.) Two sisters in South Carolina make a relish of Jerusalem artichokes from a family recipe. They market it through a local gourmet shop. The jars never get on the shelves, there are so many advance orders, many placed more than a year ahead.

Getting Started:

This is specialized, not mass production, so your best distribution is either direct to customers or through gourmet shops, local or nearby. Selling direct to your own customers is simpler in some ways—you can control the volume of production more easily, can raise or lower the price at your own discretion—but you have the problem of individual deliveries, either by your car or station wagon, or, if the product is not too large, perhaps by mail. Also, if you sell through a gourmet shop, you have the prestige of the shop's name, access to the shop's customers, and the owner can recommend your product to customers, thus giving you free publicity, and you can share in the shop's advertising on a pro rata basis.

If you decide to go it independently, perhaps your best way to start is by spreading the word that your product is available, tell the members of local clubs, religious groups, all your friends and acquaintances, and take orders. A word of caution: Be very sure that you do not take more orders than you can fill. A customer disappointed in this way is too often a customer lost. Later on, when you have perfected the smooth flow of your product and can confidently rely on so many pieces at such and such a time, you can begin to advertise in local media. (See Chapter III.)

Here is a project that can be developed into a mail order business. If you feel you can handle such an increase, begin to extend your advertising, little by little, into national publications, such as the syndicated Sunday magazine sections of newspapers.

The Cash Flow:

First expenditures for this business are low, covering mainly the ingredients of your recipe. Then advertising enters the budget, expanding with growth. Delivery expenses should be considered, low if you sell through shops, higher if you make your own deliveries.

The charge, of course, depends on the product, whether it is a smoked ham, a box of cookies, something perishable like a pie, or whether it is concocted of every day ingredients or calls for exotics. In a specialized product like this, try for a mark-up of 100%.

HOMEMADE BREAD

The Idea:

In these ecological days, old-fashioned skills, like the baking of bread at home, are much to the fore. Almost everyone loves homemade bread, but the difficulty is that almost no one has the time, patience, and know-how to make it. If you want to take advantage of the general inertia in this respect, combined with the general wish to enjoy the nutritional and gustatory benefits of homemade bread, a good part-time, home-based business can be yours.

Getting Started:

First, you should take stock of your kitchen, with emphasis on a reliable oven. Then you need a tried and tested recipe, unless you already have one, perhaps handed down from grand- and great-grandparents. If you are seeking such a recipe, here is one recommended by the wife of a United States Judge. This lady is famed for her toothsome homemade bread. She, herself, does not sell it but her loaves are in great demand to draw patrons to church and charity fund-raising affairs. Here is her recipe, which is for four loaves:

Bread—And How I Make It

1 yeast cake
2 teaspoons sugar
3 tablespoons lukewarm water

Crumble yeast in large mixing bowl, add water and sugar, and set aside.

Then measure:

2 cups sweet milk into 1-quart saucepan and let it come to a boil. Remove from flame and add:

1 teaspoon salt
½ cup shortening (I use Oleo, 1 stick)
½ cup sugar

Dissolve sugar and salt in milk, add shortening, and cover to stand until cool—or at least lukewarm.

When this mixture is cool, add it to the bowl of yeast, then add:

2 eggs
8 cups flour

Mix well. Grease top, cover with waxed paper, and let rise until double. Punch down (I slash it through several times with a long knife) and let rise again.

After the second "rise" knead down again and then divide into four equal parts, kneading each one until all air is out of each piece. Then let them "rest" for ten minutes (so that the bread will not be coarse), knead down again, and put each piece in greased loaf pan. Let rise until double—then put in pre-heated 300° oven and bake for 1 hour and 10 minutes. Turn out on cake rack at once.

For only two loaves, use half of everything except yeast —still use one yeast cake.

For whole wheat bread, use this same recipe but use *2 cups* of white flour and *6 cups* of *whole wheat* flour. ½ cup of wheat germ may also be added.

Try this, or your own recipe, on favored friends and for philanthropic sales. Then, when your own confidence and your friends' appetites are established, begin to take orders. Later, as your reputation grows, you can sell greater volume through arrangement with a gourmet shop. Your customers will probably pick up their own orders, although you may want to deliver the loaves to the shop yourself.

The Cash Flow:

This is very special custom-made food and, though the expenses are not great, time and skill required call for a high price, providing you with a 50% to 100% profit margin. This is not too much when compared with the charges for a run-of-the-mill loaf in the supermarket. Also, homemade bread usually has more substance and is more satisfying than the commercial product. Your advertising might begin small and grow as your business grows. Ads are useful in newspapers and other local publications, like programs of events. When you contract with the gourmet shop to sell your bread, perhaps you can also make an arrangement to share in the store's advertising.

TAKE-OUT DISHES

The Idea:

So many people have jobs, men and women, married and single, that the problem of a tasty and nourishing evening meal to round off a day's toil is often a problem.

Here is where you perhaps can help and at the same time establish an independent business. Set up your kitchen to offer take-out dishes, casseroles, quiche Lorraine, chicken and meat pies, roast or barbecued chicken, or chicken baked with cherries or peaches, ham cubed and creamed with sherry—you, as the head chef, can add to the list, on and on. Any one of these dishes, with a tossed salad, can constitute the main course of a meal. Not a run-of-the-mill, cold-cuts-and-potato-salad dinner, either, but a real treat. In fact, not only business people wanting a quick warm-up dinner, but hostesses seeking an especially good main dish for a company dinner may enter your collection of customers. At the same time, remember that not everyone goes for fancy food, so, along with the quiches and fish with French sauces, have plain dishes available, like macaroni and cheese and simple roasted chicken with dressing.

In this project, you don't deliver. People come in their own cars to pick up their dishes, which they have ordered earlier, either the previous day or before ten o'clock on the day of delivery.

Getting Started:

To begin with, you probably would supply a few customers acquired from among your friends and acquaintances. As you become more routined and experienced in the planning, marketing, and producing of the dishes, you can begin to advertise, in local newspapers, in house organs of businesses, in neighborhood publications, or on local radio and/or television, if your budget permits. A sign on your lawn helps customers identify your house.

The Cash Flow:

You need at least a 50% mark-up on these dishes. You will have to learn to figure out the costs, and do it frequently, as retail prices of ingredients fluctuate. This type of arithmetic takes some work in fractions and decimal points. It's tedious, but to master the math of your project is the only way to find your way to clear and present profit.

HEALTH FOOD STORE

The Idea:

People in the '70's are interested in health foods. This applies to young and old, although it has been found that the best buying age for such merchandise is the 20-40 bracket. The reason for the widespread interest is probably the current concern over processing and the chemical and other additives and preservatives in so many foods on grocery shelves. The result is an increase in the number of stores catering to health foods. In 1973 there were 3,000 such stores in the nation, served by some 250 manufacturers and distributors. The totals may be larger by now.

The Bank of America's *Small Business Reporter* devotes a 15-page, plus appendix, pamphlet to health food stores and differentiates between terms. "Organic" refers to a growing process as well as a final product. "Natural" describes the preparation of the food (no preservatives, emulsifiers, artificial coloring, flavorings, etc.). "Health food" covers organic, natural, and special diet foods, although not all health foods are organic or natural—for example, low sodium crackers are a must for salt free diets, yet they are neither organic nor natural.

A "natural food store" caters to dedicated organic foodists. Such a store probably does not sell organic meats and poultry, offering mostly grains, flours, nuts, seeds, teas, herbs, and dairy products, and no synthetic vitamins or mass-produced cosmetics. A "health food store" has a more varied choice of foods. Besides a complete stock of natural, organic, and health foods, there are meat, poultry and meat substitutes, natural and synthetic vitamins and food supplements, and health and beauty aids.

Getting Started:

If you feel drawn to this field, and have some knowledge of nutrition, the *Small Business Reporter* pamphlet urges also retail food experience as a background, employment in a supermarket, for instance, and emphasizes that a health food store, like all businesses, depends on the acumen and know-how of its owner. Perhaps the best beginning for anyone contemplating opening a health food store would be to send for this pamphlet, which includes discussion of the advantages and possible disadvantages of buying an established store rather than opening a new one; the necessity of preliminary market research; the importance of site location; licenses and permits; design and layout, interior and exterior; equipment costs; inventory investment; insurance; sources of financial assistance; sources of supply; government regulations; pricing; advertising and promotion; employee relations; and a list of further useful publications.

The Cash Flow:

The pamphlet gives an overall table of investment requirements for two hypothetical stores, one with annual sales of $100,000 and floor space of 1500 square feet, the other with annual sales of $250,000 and floor space of 2400 square feet, comprising opening costs, premises, and inventory. The total is $25,000 for the smaller store, $44,300 for the larger. These are 1973 figures. Operating costs are given, for the same annual sales and floor spaces, in a table of net sales, cost of goods sold, gross profit, expenses (wages, rent, advertising, etc.), with a net profit of 7% for the smaller store and 13% for the larger.

HORS D'OEUVRES FOR PARTIES

The Idea:

Hors d'oeuvres, properly prepared, glamorous to look at, delectable to taste, take time and patience in the making, plus a special flair for this creativity. Some successful caterers and hostesses have this patience and flair. Lots of party-givers have not. The have-nots in this case usually buy the appetizers to go with the drinks when they give a cocktail party. If you have skill in converting certain foodstuffs into delicious blends to ride on crackers or melba rounds, perhaps you would enjoy going into the business. There is certainly opportunity for artistry. The colors—the red and black of the caviar, yellow and white of cheeses and eggs, glossy brown of anchovies, white of lobster and crab meat, green of chopped pepper and chives—and the different fancy shapes and sizes of the hors d'oeuvres can present a picture to make a photographer reach for his camera. The kitchen sculptor can design lovely, if perishable tidbits—and, if they taste as good as they look, they will perish soon after the guests sight them.

Getting Started:

If you have this kind of talent, you know it from the

success of your own parties. If you want to commercialize, you should broaden your repertoire by studying every cookbook, standard, regional, ethnic, or ecological, that comes your way and copy out interesting new recipes of your specialty. Ask friends for recipes and gather ideas when you travel. Don't stick to hors d'oeuvres entirely; go in for dips, not the conventional dehydrated onion ones, but unusual ones found in your researches. Invent new ones and try them out.

You probably have acquaintances who will give you orders, and try dropping in on quality delis and gourmet shops and offering samples of your wares. See if they will sell them for you. A lot of business can result from such contacts. If you want to run small ads, have them placed on the society page.

You will probably always work to order and make the hors d'oeuvres on the day of the party. Some dips, of course, can be made up ahead of time, perhaps sold in jars.

The Cash Flow:

In computing your profits for this work, first list all your expenses, inclusive of: product cost, delivery, utilities (electricity and gas), your time, personnel cost (even if it's your son, daughter, or husband!). Total these expenses. Add on a profit ranging from 50% to 100%, depending on competition, difficulty of preparation, uniqueness, etc. Thus, you assure yourself a good *net* profit for your endeavors.

CELEBRITY COOKBOOK

The Idea:

Are you creative in culinary art? Are you good at thinking up, testing, and serving original recipes, or improvements and variations on standard recipes?

If so, perhaps you owe it to yourself to assemble these recipes and write a cookbook.

But if you do, you need to find a publisher, and if there is a division of publishing that is plentifully supplied, it is that featuring cookbooks. You need a gimmick, and the publisher needs a gimmick, to direct attention to your special book.

One way to do this is to identify your book with a popular personality. Actors, musicians, television figures, athletes, authors, dancers, wives of prominent politicians, all like to have their names before the public. In a nice way, of course. And what could be nicer than association with good food? So-and-So's Favorite Recipes as a title might be just the way to induce people to buy your book.

Getting Started:

How to get the chosen celebrity to lend his (her) name to your manuscript? The best way is to find out who manages the personality. A celebrity almost certainly has a manager, or a reasonable facsimile, like a literary agent for an author. Contact the management with your suggestion. If you have a degree in Home Economics, here is the place to stress it. Also be sure to mention any recipes you might have had published in local papers or featured at local banquets, food sales, or in cooking courses. Give some description of the kind of recipes you favor and say why your type of cuisine is appropriate to the celebrity—Southern regional dishes for a blues singer from Alabama, or hearty stews and plain but toothsome cakes and pies for a rugged masculine actor. If you don't succeed with one celebrity, try others. Once you have the go-ahead to attach the celebrity's name to your book, the management might even help you find a publisher.

The Cash Flow:

Your expenses are not high—correspondence with the management, if you can't contact them in person, and perhaps letters to publishers, plus the cost of having your manuscript typed, if you can't do that yourself in professional style. If you can type it yourself, you will save a bundle.

Income, of course, depends on whether you get, first, a celebrity, and, second, a publisher. If you succeed in bringing out the book, you get a royalty on each copy sold. Depending on the agreement, you might have to share royalties with the celebrity, but perhaps he might consider he has received value in having his name featured.

TEST KITCHEN

The Idea:

Many food manufacturers and importers depend a great deal on recipes to promote their products, especially new or "improved" products. At least, they hope the new process improves the flavor of the spaghetti or the canned fruit, or whatever. To make as sure as they can, before a product goes on the market, it is tested, in new and standard recipes.

Here is where you might put your kitchen to commercial use. If there are one or more plants in your vicinity turning out foods, or if there are importers and food brokers nearby, they are the ones to contact and offer your kitchen and your services for recipe testing.

Getting Started:

First, you might ask your local Chamber of Commerce for a list of prospective clients, or you could look them up in the Yellow Pages. The first way may be better, since, besides giving you the requested list, the Chamber of Commerce will probably discuss your project with you and make pertinent suggestions.

Next, a short, concise letter outlining the service you are prepared to give should go to each name on the list. At the end of the letter, say you will telephone them soon and hope for an appointment to talk further about the matter. Some of these firms will have their own test kitchens but some may find your idea interesting enough to give you an interview. Here is where you do the real selling, inviting your prospective client to visit your kitchen to see that it is adequately equipped and large enough to bring several people there for testings, if necessary.

The Cash Flow:

A minimum fee of $50 is charged for each "test." Initial expenses are practically nil, only the postage and stationery for the letters and the gas or carfare to keep appointments. Advertising is not necessary. You have a limited group of customers with whom you will keep close and constant contact. You work from home so there is no rent.

GOURMET SHOP

The Idea:

Special foods—ethnic, regional, nostalgic—are becoming more and more popular as travel and communications make people's appetites more sophisticated. If your neighborhood or town has no gourmet shop, why not consider the idea of opening a small one yourself?

Such a project need not take up much space. You need only a corner in your garage, in part of your basement, or in any room in your house that is accessible, has generous wall space for shelves, and can be made to look bright and attractive. If you do not want to operate from home, remember that in renting you need minimum space. For location, think of the people you hope to make customers and ask yourself if they pass that way. And be sure to check with your lawyer as to whether you need a license.

Getting Started:

If this shop is your choice for a business, you probably know something about foods, but perhaps know little about the wholesale market. Contact the National Association for

Specialty Foods Trade, 30 East 42nd Street, New York, N.Y. 10017. They have 150 members, either importers or manufacturers of specialty foods, including confections, baked goods, canned and packaged foods from all sections of our own country and from all over the world. Literature and price lists are also available. The Association holds shows twice a year, one in the East, the other in the West, where you can see fine food exhibits by the hundreds and attend helpful seminars for retailers. The Association's magazine lists many of their members' products.

In a small store, such as yours, you would do well to stick to canned and packaged items and avoid the perishables, like cheese, which needs special refrigeration and has a limited shelf life. Baked goods are only advisable if you can bake your own or sell the products of some neighbor's oven. Canned and packaged goods require no refrigeration and do not spoil, and their number is legion—exotic meats, fish, fowl, and game; choice and varied vegetables and fruits; jams and jellies; olives and pickles; cookies and fruitcakes; mixes for cakes, pies, desserts, pancakes and crepes; teas, coffees, cocoa, soft drink and cocktail mixes. The cans and packages, in their bright containers, make a colorful display in themselves.

The Cash Flow:

Advertising costs can be kept low, perhaps held to a regularly appearing small ad on the food page of your newspaper and occasional good will advertising in programs for high school plays and other events. Direct mail is one of the best ways to advertise this kind of store. Send out postcards every month or so, announcing some new kind of food or drink, or a new line of ethnic foods, say, Mexican or Scandinavian.

A woman who has put this plan into successful operation suggests a budget for ordering your original stock of about $1,000, with a profit of 40%. And, she warns, reorder judiciously. Your shelves should never look meagerly supplied.

9.

WRITING—THE PEN IS MIGHTIER THAN THE SWORD—MORE PROFITABLE, TOO

ARTICLE WRITING

The Idea:

Trade and business magazines offer a market to the alert writer who would like to earn extra income from articles about the current commercial scene. If you have a flair for such writing, have a clear, concise style suitable to factual reporting, this could be your medium.

Getting Started:

At your public library you can consult the Ayer Directory of Publications and look up the names and addresses of trade papers under whatever categories interest you. Then look around you for material. Does your neighborhood grocery use clever signs? Does your favorite bakery employ a special gimmick to attract customers? Are there merchants in your locality whose enterprise and merchandising methods are outstanding? Are there clever and unusual window displays in nearby stores? Any of these could offer the subject of an interview with the proprietor and a story about his services.

Select your store and its special feature, then write a letter to the editor of an appropriate magazine, outlining briefly and effectively the article you propose. Suggest pictures. If you cannot take photographs yourself, the store will generally be glad to arrange for some. If the first editor you contact is not interested, try other publications in the field. When you receive encouragement, that is, when an editor says he would like to see your article (he probably won't commit himself any farther), go to the store with the letter, get your material in detail, arrange for the pictures—and write the article and hope the editor likes it.

After a publication has bought several of your stories, the editor may give you assignments to visit stores and manufacturing plants to get stories.

The Cash Flow:

Trade magazines usually pay five to ten cents a word for free lance articles and $5 to $25 for accompanying photographs.

GHOST WRITER

The Idea:

How many public personalities write their own speeches? Their own memoirs? Sssh. Don't ask.

Someone prominent enough, like the President of the United States, has a crew of writers working on his utterances. However, there are many lesser lights who would be satisfied with one competent ghost writer.

If you are that able phantom, and you don't mind having your immortal prose attributed to another, then you should be in line for such a career. You may be kept busy by one client, but if you need more, your prospects are legion, not only politicians but inarticulate scientists and inventors, heads of trade associations, even officials of Boards of Education, who perhaps can do their own writing but simply haven't the time.

Getting Started:

Getting started as a ghost writer is not too easy. Unlike satisfied clients in other fields, yours may be reluctant to acknowledge they need your service and thus be in a position to recommend you. Small ads of ghost writers, with replies to be directed to a box number, are fairly frequent in Sunday magazine and book review sections of big newspapers and in writers' magazines. If you are known to publishers as a good, flexible writer, these editors may recommend you to someone whose experience and background are bookworthy but who lacks the means of expression through words and has no idea of how to organize material. Another way is to volunteer in political campaigns, get known to busy politicians and work yourself in as a speech and press release writer.

The Cash Flow:

This is probably a part-time job, and the pay will have to be according to the importance of the client and the book, article, or speech to be written.

GREETING CARD VERSE

The Idea:

Is yours a rhyming mind? Do thoughts and fancies take metrical form for you? Are you clever at putting your sentiments into verse and do you instinctively give your lines the correct number of feet? Not everyone can do this, but if verse comes trippingly off your pen, why not capitalize on it? Get the writers' magazines and check the market for poetry. You will probably find that the best paying verse is the greeting card kind.

Getting Started:

Don't think that this is an easy market. If you decide to

write greeting card verse, you are in competition with old pros who have been turning it out for years and furthermore keep up with what the publishers want. According to an article in a writers' trade publication, in the '70's the greeting card industry wants new and different ideas, rather than the conventional.

There are many categories of greeting cards, including Contemporary, Conventional, Cute, Everyday (like birthday cards), Humorous, Inspirational, Risque, Mechanical (contains an action of some kind), Pop-up, Promotion (a series with a common feature, like Classique's Barnyard Buddies), Studio, Soft-line (gentle me-to-you messages), Topical (dealing with ecology, perhaps), Seasonal. You do not need to write poetry necessarily, anymore, provided you can command what *The Writer's Handbook* calls "rhythmic, readable prose."

Contributors no longer confine themselves to suggestions for cards. The greeting card houses welcome ideas for books, puzzles, games, party items, calendars, posters, all the supplementary things you see in card shops now.

If you want to stick to thoughts for cards, for the "conventional" verse, submit your lines, neatly printed, on either 4" x 6" or 3" x 5" slips or file cards. For humorous or studio ideas, either use file cards or fold sheets of paper into card dummies, print neatly or type words as they would appear on the actual dummy card. Put your name and address on the back of each dummy or card, along with a code, like 1, 2, 3, etc., so that the editor can refer to a particular idea when he writes to you. Be sure to include a stamped return envelope for rejects.

All these and further instructions and guidance are found in the trade publications, notably *The Writer's Handbook* and *Writer's Market*, which are available in most public and reference libraries. Major greeting card houses get out regular market letters, stressing current needs.

The Cash Flow:

If and when you make a sale, the recompense varies with the publisher. In the writers' reference books mentioned above are included lists of greeting card publishers and their rates of pay, ranging from $5 to $100 and up.

RURAL SCENIC BOOKLET

The Idea:

Most localities like to attract tourists and also most localities have spots worth a tourist's visit. A woman in a small Pennsylvania town got the idea of publicizing nearby scenic beauties in a booklet to be sold at airports, bus stations, motel desks, and the county's newsstands.

Getting Started:

To begin with, she did thorough research, listing those spots with which she was familiar and checking the library and newspaper office for others. She visited these spots in her car and sketched maps of how to get to each. Wherever she could, she secured pictures. A short description of each place of interest was written in as intriguing a style as she could summon.

With this material, she consulted several printers and selected the best offer for price and layout. With the dummy of her publication in hand, she went to local business owners, told of her plan to print the booklet, and sold advertising to many of them.

The Cash Flow:

She sold advertising space for $10 per inch, $25 a column, or $165 a page, with the centerspread priced at $150. After paying the printer and counting up her advertising revenue, she found she could sell the pamphlet at twenty five cents each and come out well on the right side of the ledger.

This pamphlet has been so successful that its editor has issued several annual revised and expanded editions.

PROOFREADING

The Idea:

Good eyesight, better than average concentration, and knowledge of grammar and spelling make the proofreader. Able workers in this field are not common, and printers are usually glad to find one and will often let such a reader work at home, if that is preferred.

Material to be read and corrected includes not only the long articles and feature stories of a newspaper or the chapters of a book. Job printers—and a local newspaper is frequently a job printer, too—get out pamphlets, throw-aways, programs, posters, mailing pieces, financial reports, invitations, stationery, a variety of items. Some of these have few words, but it is all the more vital that every letter and figure be correct. A wrong digit in an address may make a piece of publicity useless. The wrong letter in a word, or reversed letters, can make a statement ridiculous or change its meaning altogether. Try changing "now" to "not," or "sacred" to "scared," "dear" to "deaf" or "dead." The proofreader assumes an important responsibility; there is often more than one proofreader, so that the possibility of errors is thus cut down, but there are instances when time is of the essence and only one proofreader is available.

So a proofreader must be, first, aware of the importance of accuracy and, second, able to accept the fact that no one is infallible and an occasional mistake happens, even when there is a staff of excellent proofreaders to share the guilt.

Getting Started:

If you have had no experience and wish to learn proofreading, the mechanics of the craft are not difficult. A chart of proofreader's marks can be obtained from any publisher or printer. When you pick it up, tell the printer that you are interested in doing proofreading and ask him for some extra proofs to practice on. After you think you are skilled enough, go to printing and publishing houses and offer your services. If you earn a reputation for reliability, you will probably not lack for work.

The Cash Flow:

Expenses for the job, if it is done at home, are minimal, involving carfare or gas going to and from the employer, or postage if the completed work is to be mailed in.

The pay ranges from about $4 an hour to $8 an hour for a highly skilled and experienced worker.

CONFESSION STORIES

The Idea:

With the short story market much dwindled, due to the fact that so many general magazines are no more, one class of such fiction is still in short supply. The editors of the confession magazines are eager for new material. Some twenty-five confession magazines are published and new authors submitting the required sort of writing are welcomed.

Getting Started:

What is the right material? Can you supply it? An article by Jean Jackson in *Writer's Handbook*, advised the author interested in this market to survey her readership. Readers of confession stories are almost all women. Their general age range is 13-35, their education high school or under, their occupations something like typist, dressmaker, salesgirl, or housewife. They are married or in love with hotel clerks, factory workers, or holders of small white collar jobs. They are interested in problems that they might have themselves.

Now, if these statistics give you a superiority complex, stop right there. Neither editors nor readers in this field will tolerate writing down and can sense it immediately.

The stories are in the first person and deal with some mistake in conduct or point of view on the part of the protagonist. The mistake, persisted in over a period, brings unhappiness to the narrator or to someone she loves. She perceives her error and goes about undoing the damage, as far as possible.

Does this sound simple? Such a formula represents only the bare bones of a creation. Your best way to learn this style of writing is to buy an armful of confession magazines, study them, and try to learn their patterns and techniques. Then try your hand at writing a story or two and submit them to editors. You may not succeed in selling your first efforts, but confession editors are good about sometimes returning a manuscript with a letter of constructive criticism, rather than the usual printed rejection slip.

The Cash Flow:

This venture, like all free lance writing, is speculative. It may be a long time before you get cash returns, if you ever do. But once you get started, confession stories can bring you substantial recompense. A Westchester matron earns an annual income well up in the five figures by writing for the confession market. By now, she is known to the editors, who sometimes assign her special plots to work out.

RADIO SCRIPTS

The Idea:

Most localities have small radio stations supported by

advertising. Here may be a market for a writer who is enterprising and has good, flexible skills. If you can compose a clever, appealing, short ad script for a merchant of your town, you have a good chance of selling it to him for broadcast. A fresh idea, an individual twist, will make his ad stand out from the usual dreary drone.

Also, most of these small stations are looking for material to keep their listeners tuned in to them, rather than to the big competition. If you write a series of skits based on the history of your town or state, or of some well known figures of the vicinity, it is probable that the station will help you get sponsors from among the town's business owners. If there are several sponsors, the expenses of the project, that is, the station's fee plus your charge, will not be heavy on anyone.

Getting Started:

Preparation for this work might begin with becoming thoroughly familiar with the broadcasts of your local station or stations ads, news, music, and features. You want your material to be in line with their output and policies, but with something distinctive and new about it. Listen to the ads and time them, so that you can suit copy to the seconds allowed for it.

When you have some ideas and thoughts you want to follow up, go to the station and ask for some old scripts so you can learn the form. If you know the station owner, or someone who works for the station, it helps but is not essential. Good ideas are acceptable, whether they come from an acquaintance or not.

The Cash Flow:

No rent, no advertising here. Just leg work, contacting station owners, merchants, and subjects for features or people who can give you interesting local history, past and present.

Income from this type of work depends on your writing creativity and speed. Average payment is $20 to $50 for a thirty-second ad script. Profitability ensues from the repeat patronage, and the multiplicity of clients you can obtain in your area. Thus, earnings mount. Suddenly, you have a flourishing "growth" business.

NURSE ROMANCES

The Idea:

A certain kind of literary market is open for short novels with a medical background, dealing with the adventures (sentimental adventures mostly, of course) of a pure, young nurse. Titles like Flight Nurse, A Nurse's Dilemma, Nurse at Scary Manor and so on are found among the paperbacks on newsstands.

Getting Started:

Can you write in this medium? It's a long shot, but if you want to make a try the first thing to do is to buy and read all these books that you can, thus absorbing the style and content that is wanted. To broaden your knowledge of hospitals and medical lore generally, read all the doctors' columns in the newspapers, watch the many television programs and soap operas with a medical slant. Talk to any nurses among your own acquaintances and they will probably suggest textbooks to read that are not too technical for a layman.

Then make a list of the names and addresses of the publishing houses that issue nurse sagas. Think out a suitable plot, write two chapters and an outline (the chapters need not be the first two in your completed book; you can choose any), and send it to one of the publishers.

The melancholy truth is that the chances are greatly in favor of your receiving your masterpiece back with a polite thanks but no thanks. Then on to the next publisher on your list. Eventually, you might get a cautious letter of encouragement somewhere along the line, expressing interest in seeing your full manuscript. If the publisher should find the resulting work satisfactory, after rewrite, then you will break into print. After you have had at least one manuscript accepted, you can probably get an agent who will market your writing. Here, again, you must be careful. But that is another story.

The Cash Flow:

There is little invested here but lots and lots of time, plus quite a bit of stationery, postage, and return postage (don't forget to enclose the postage for the manuscript to be sent back to you, should it be rejected). It is to be hoped that you can type your own manuscript, since the price of hiring a typist will run up the cost of this speculative activity out of all proportion.

The (possible) financial returns are not bad. Various publishers pay various prices, comprising advance payment followed by royalty on copies sold. Such novels do not make the best seller lists but you might well realize several thousand dollars per book.

MAKE-BELIEVE PEN PAL

The Idea:

A writer with time on her hands tried a long shot experiment, which paid off.

She inserted an ad in newspapers offering to write letters from imaginary correspondents to persons desiring to receive such mail. The response surprised her. Shut-ins, aged and lonely people, spinsters denied romance, and armchair travelers were among the people interested in her services. She now writes letters to a variety of clients, from phantom children, lovers, spouses, worldly counselors, mellow professors, globe trotters. The recipient specifies how often the letters are to be received and renews his "subscription" at agreed upon intervals.

The writer feels that these letters fill voids in the lives of her clients in a more personal way than is offered by watching television or reading novels.

Getting Started:

Would you like to go into a writing project like this? Have you imagination, knowledge of character, a gift for different modes of expression for the different personalities mirrored in the letters? You should also have what the theatre calls empathy, that is, ability to identify with another, in this case with your clients, who must have some deep need or they would not be reaching out for fantasy in this way.

If you want to try your hand, insert small ads not only in local newspapers but in national publications like *Saturday Review* and *Popular Mechanics,* both of which carry out-of-the-ordinary ads. You will probably get responses, which can be built into a clientele.

The Cash Flow:

Your expenses are mainly advertising, along with postage and stationery. Your capital is your time and ingenuity.

Probably the best way to charge is by the month, with a letter a week promised, or one every two weeks. $25 for the first, $15 for the second arrangement is reasonable. When a client has tried your service and likes it, he can contract for longer periods at special rates.

COLLECTION LETTERS

The Idea:

The world is full of people who can pay their bills, and

mean to pay their bills, but are in no hurry about it. Business owners must collect from these people but are loath to offend them. Of course, there are accounts that never will be paid. Sometimes it is the "can't get blood out of a turnip" principle, other times it is because the debtor is constitutionally adapted to running up bills, ignoring such obligations, promising to pay when confronted, and then starting the process all over again.

Still, a large proportion of delinquents will pay eventually if they are not allowed to forget all about it.

If you have patience, fortitude, and a liking for detective work in tracing people who would like to disappear, you may be a good one-woman collection agency. It is not a bad idea to have worked for a collection organization. You learn recognized techniques. However, if you go out on your own, you will probably develop your own methods.

Getting Started:

A young clerk has instituted a profitable sideline by writing a series of six letters designed to bring old accounts to collection, beginning with a polite reminder, then going on to remonstrance, finally to stern threat of legal recourse. The last letter offers 20% reduction for immediate settlement. These letters are written so that they can be adapted to the individuals to whom they apply and to their business or profession. In some cases, this collector scraps the form letters and makes an entirely new approach.

How did the young clerk begin? By getting up a list of merchants and writing them letters describing his service. The response was small at first but this is the sort of business that grows with perseverance and experience.

The Cash Flow:

Such an activity can be operated from home, since only a

desk and typewriter are required. The clients provide the stationery and postage. Advertising in the Yellow Pages is a good idea and, of course, success for one client will bring recommendation to other creditors.

Perhaps the charge might be one-third of the amount collected. Thus, for a collection of $1,500, the collector gets $500.

10.

OPPORTUNITIES FOR THE ORGANIZER

MANAGEMENT CONSULTANT

The Idea:

The profession of management consultant, a relatively new one, is akin to the practice of medicine in that businesses that are ailing call for its services, and some wise businesses don't wait until they are "sick" but retain a management consultant firm on a "preventive" basis.

The consultant should be familiar with all phases of business administration or be a specialist in one particular field. There are not many women management consultants, for one reason because few women have as yet been given the opportunity to acquire the necessary know-how. So, if you should decide to go into this activity, you may encounter some discrimination here and there.

Getting Started:

This is work that calls for background, in education and experience. A Bachelor of Science or Business Administration degree, while perhaps not absolutely necessary, certainly helps in getting a job with an established management consultant firm and starting to acquire experience. This sort of beginning may not be rigidly called for, but is certainly advisable.

When you start out on your own, it might be well to do so along with several associates who specialize in fields other than yours. Be sure to consult your lawyer as to any license or permit necessary in your state. You do not have to pass exams like a doctor or lawyer but the consultants' associations stress standards of ethics. There are a number of these associations, most located in New York City, with one in Wisconsin. From your previous employment with a management consultant firm you will know of these associations and which one you would like to join.

The Cash Flow:

To save rent, you might start your own business from your home, if you can spare the space. There will be initial expense enough for the license (if required), office furniture, reference books, secretarial service, stationery, telephone, and advertising.

Fees for management consultant services are far from fixed, varying from section to section and governed, too, by the size and nature of the client's business, but a price-by-the-day is usual. Your major clients may retain you on an annual basis so as to have your advice at any time. Such clients, of course, should be assiduously cultivated, and close and constant relationship maintained.

FASHION SHOWS

The Idea:

If you live in a suburb or a middle-sized city, and if you have a flair for fashion and yet don't care for a behind-the-counter saleswoman's job or a buyer's career, perhaps your talents are suited to putting on fashion shows for the local department stores.

Getting Started:

To begin with, have you a pleasant voice and clear diction? Have you exceptional organizing ability?

To prepare, you need to recall all the shows you have attended and arrange to see all you can currently, including some offered by the big stores in major cities. Such attendance demonstrates the spectacle from an audience-eye view, and you can hear the commentator speak and decide how your voice would sound if you took over the role. It all seems effortless, the tall, beautiful models drifting across the runway, displaying stunning garments, the tape recorded music melodious and serene, the talk appropriate and sparked with charm.

Backstage is another matter, and you had better take part in some shows as a dresser for the models in your preliminary training. Here turn the unseen wheels within wheels of the intricate organization of the show. Someone, probably the commentator, has worked long and hard. First she worked with the store's staff to make sure proper advertising and publicity heralded the day. Then, before the actual event she made sure the stage or runway was clean, properly lighted, and the backdrop arranged; that the operators of the lighting and of the tape recorder were reliable and adequately cued. She has either hired the right professional models to show the line, or, if the models are nonprofessionals, she has survived the difficult' diplomacy of trying to get the right, or as near right as possible, model for a gown or coat without offending some important but inappropriate aspirant.

Still more vital, she has assembled, in proper order, all the garments and accessories, so that the dressers, standing in their cubicles, can help the models change without ever pausing to locate the right shoes, scarf, stole, or jewelry to complete a costume. Oh, yes, and the shoes for each model to change into must be the proper size.

Before you charge for your service as a director of fashion shows, better put on a number of such events for your club or charity.

The Cash Flow:

To enter into this activity, you need only time, not much actual cash. Your contacts with prospective clients will probably be made in person, or, when you can afford the expenditure, mail campaign, enclosing a multigraphed page of favorable newspaper reviews of your most outstanding shows.

Perhaps you will put on fashion shows as a supplementary activity rather than a full-time business, since stores do not give style shows every day or even every month. However, if you want to give all your time to the work, you might consider trying to interest stores not only in your city but in nearby centers. This would entail travel and living expenses to add to your budget.

Charges would no doubt vary, depending on the section of the country, size of the city or cities, and type of stores. Perhaps $50 a day for the time necessary for organization, $100 for the actual day of the show.

SET UP SALES CONFERENCES

The Idea:

Are you good, *really* good, at organization? Can you set up motel reservations; a transportation system; interesting meals; for a sizable group? Can you cope, efficiently and without getting wild-eyed, with a minor hitch in proceedings and keep it from growing into a major crisis? If so, look around and see if you know of a small manufacturing business that is, or might be, considering a conference and training session for dealers and salesmen.

Getting Started:

Offer your services to such firms to arrange the living and entertainment schedule to mesh in with the meetings.

This sort of work has the virtue of never being dull, right from registration and the get-acquainted cocktail party. If sessions can be held in the motel where the reservations have been made, it simplifies matters immeasurably. However, perhaps the sessions must be held at the plant. At any rate, there will be visits to the plant.

To get all persons to where they should be at the proper time is a challenge, involving collecting them, quietly and diplomatically, from dining room and bar, interrupting reunions and breaking up cliques, and getting them into their cars. If special meals are part of the treat, it is well to have a good, long time at the restaurant, with allowance for their being late through no fault of their own—say, an unexpectedly interesting and extended question and answer period. Chefs should be prepared for this and menus drawn up accordingly.

A program for wives is generally required. Here, if possible, enlist the help of the wives of plant officials in providing cars to drive to local scenic spots; suggestions for shopping; and teas and luncheons.

At the farewell banquet you will probably be moving only on momentum, but if you have kept the schedule going with reasonable smoothness, with disasters avoided and their threat not even known to the visitors, then word will probably get around and you will have offers to plan and conduct programs for other conferences.

The Cash Flow:

No advertising necessary here. Cultivate contacts. Keep an ear to the ground and when you hear of sales conferences coming up, drive over and see the executives in charge, cite past successes and suggest that they let you do similar work for them.

Pay should be good, at least $100 a day, plus telephone, gas, and your other expenses.

MINI-AVON

The Idea:

One of the smartest things you can learn is to learn from the successful. The minis, while not on as large a scale, can learn a lot from the maxis. Take Avon Calling, one of the biggest successes going. Why not try a mini-Avon?

Getting Started:

In the Yellow Pages of the telephone book can be found cosmetic manufacturers who will furnish a formula for a private label specialist. Shop around, find an aid for skin care, or a skin or lip coloring that you really like. Consult with the chemist to discover what it will truly do—help to correct a dry skin condition, temporarily smooth wrinkles, feed the skin, or give tints that appeal to you; all this so that you can believe in your line and honestly promote it.

Attractive packaging and its cost is another important feature. A container and box distinctive in design and color will point up quality. Here again, pore over the Yellow Pages under "Packaging." You will probably find so many firms that breaking down the list to the ones that have a design and art department, and at the same time are interested in a small account, may be quite a task. But carry on, select a few firms, go and see them, if possible; if not, negotiate by letter and telephone. If you find an organization to understand your needs and supply you economically, one battle in your campaign is won.

Study Avon's advertising and pricing and, as far as is practical and within your means, do likewise. Locally, that is. Take ads on local television and radio stations, in local and neighborhood newspapers and in programs for theatrical and other events. Go from door to door yourself to sell, if you are good at that sort of thing. If not, pay someone else to do it.

If your product is good, people will like it. More and more promotional ideas will come to you. Who knows? Eventually you might be only moderately mini.

The Cash Flow:

This needs a considerable starting budget. You must pay the chemist and the packaging people, and then there is your introductory advertising. If you have a door-to-door salesperson, try to get him or her to work on commission.

Your charges should be based on the cost per unit of your products.

COMMUNITY EXCHANGE

The Idea:

In these unisex days, let's turn the old-fashioned Women's Exchange into a Community Exchange. If you have a barn, or an outside garage with spare space, or a big room in your house that you can devote to other than family use, and if you know people skilled, really skilled, in handicrafts, ceramics, baking, candy-making, needlepoint, quilting, painting, sculpting small figures, scarf or tie designing and creation, cabinet making, or the like, perhaps you would enjoy gathering together an attractive and varied stock of their output and presenting these wares for sale on commission.

Women will probably be the most numerous of those responding, but you may be surprised at how many men, and even children, will contribute creations.

Getting Started:

You need, first, to have a large number of creative people on call. They are your suppliers. Some you probably know. Others can be located through the ones you do know and through friends. Art schools, craft centers, and senior citizen organizations will be glad to suggest their star pupils. You will have to develop and concentrate on diplomacy because you will not find all offerings suitable and, of course, you want to refuse without offending (if possible!).

It is important to display the objects attractively. This is a talent in itself and if you have a friend or associate more gifted in this way than you, perhaps you should ask for help. Avoid clutter, try for balance, that is, not too many heavy objects on one side of the room and only little ones on the other. Watch color effects, aim for bright eye-catching contrasts.

The Cash Flow:

You will need to advertise consistently with small, characteristic ads, say with your own logo, in newspapers on the home and decorating pages, especially at Christmas and other holiday seasons. Local radio and television publicity would be good, if you can afford it. Try for feature stories and pictures in your newspapers and for a television showing. Announce, through direct mail, special showings, perhaps seasonal, with tea and cookies served. Get one of your artists to design a striking sign for your lawn or window.

All this means that your advertising budget is not small, and if you can't conduct this enterprise from home or on your own grounds, you will have rent, too.

You should charge 50% commission, with an agreement to be signed by all whose work you present.

This is not an enterprise that will put you in the upper income brackets, but it may bring you a comfortable return that will increase as community interest grows.

CHILDREN'S APPAREL EXCHANGE

The Idea:

Even if you have no children of your own, you have certainly observed how quickly a babe in arms becomes a creeper, a creeper a toddler, and a toddler a walking, running child; and all the time the child is getting bigger. This process of getting bigger continues for years and years.

Meantime, with every phase, children need new clothes, and the phases come so fast that they do not have time to wear out clothes. Thus, the parents are periodically left with (almost) good-as-new shoes, shirts, sweaters, socks, overalls, etc., that are of no use to the original wearer, whose parents must go to considerable expense in buying clothes for the phase that's just been entered.

This biological phenomenon—that of a child's growth—may offer you an opportunity for free enterprise. You might start a children's apparel exchange, either buying the outgrown clothing and selling it to a parent whose child has just reached the proper size; or you can take it on a consignment basis, to be sold, if possible, in a given time, with commission to you, or returned to the supplying parent. Only actual experience will show which, in your case, is the better plan. However, you can probably count on a supplier many times becoming a purchaser, that is, a mother comes in with clothes her four-year-old has outgrown, you accept them, and she then looks around her to see if you have a replacement on hand in the new size.

Getting Started:

You need to know a lot of young mothers and be located

in a spot easily accessible to them. This enterprise can be carried on in your barn or basement. It needs room, and if you cannot spare space from your home, you should look for low-rent accommodations.

Such a business is usually made known by word of mouth, but you can write letters to parents and put an ad in the classified section of newspapers.

You need not take as much trouble for display as you would in a fashion store, but your quarters should always be spotless and the little clothes assorted into sizes.

The Cash Flow:

If you can run the business from home, you have no rent, but your budget includes what advertising you do. You need bins and a rack or two. Perhaps you can get the latter second hand.

Most important, if you obtain the clothes on consignment, there is no usual "inventory" cost. You display them in your exchange; if you sell them, you obtain your designated sales commission. If you don't sell them, you merely have them picked up by the donor-customer.

Sales commission for an exchange of this type is generally 30%, a markup that allows a good earnings potential, too.

In stocking the clothes and pricing them for sale, you, your suppliers, and customers must remember that such prices are expected to be low. People coming into your store come for bargains. Otherwise, they would buy their children's clothing new.

11.

PUTTING YOUR OFFICE KNOW-HOW TO WORK

BOOKKEEPING SERVICE

The Idea:

If you have had office experience as a bookkeeper, and liked the work, would you like to adapt your skill to a free lance activity with growth possibilities? How about acting as part-time bookkeeper to several nearby businesses that are too small to hire one full time? Most owners of such small stores or offices do not have the training or inclination themselves to do an efficient job of keeping accounts and are all too happy to turn such matters over to a competent, if intermittent, helper.

Getting Started:

To start, check your locality for likely clients—small grocers, boutiques, pet shops, restaurants, offices of doctors, dentists, architects—and make a list. Contact your prospects in person, by telephone, or by letter and suggest your service. About now, you will probably discover that a bookkeeping service is a good activity for two people. If you have a friend who is free to join in with you and would like to undertake the solicitation and contacting end while you do the actual book-keeping, this association might work well. A one-woman project has its advantages but is likely not only to be lonely but to accumulate too much work for one person. The right partner can make the routine more congenial, as well as enabling easier expansion of the business.

The Cash Flow:

To settle on the proper charge, you might call a few bookkeeping services listed in the Yellow Pages to discover the going rate. If there are no such services listed, talk to the prospects and settle on a charge, either by the hour or for a period of time.

STENOGRAPHER AND NOTARY PUBLIC

The Idea:

Have you knowledge of shorthand and typing and either are or would like to be a notary public? Thus equipped, you can, if your ambition lies in that direction, set up your own public stenographic service from home.

Getting Started:

If you are not a notary public, get in touch with your state registration department, comply with their procedure, and receive your stamp and seal. Unless you are already familiar with legal forms, it would be well to study commercial law books, or take a course in legal stenography, and thus be prepared to compose as well as type and notarize papers required by your clients.

After this preparation, put a sign "Notary Public" in your window, arrange your desk, typewriter, and plain stationery, and wait for business. Some clients will want only to dictate letters, or perhaps speeches, which do not require notarization, but when the latter is required it is vital that you are able to supply it.

Your sign in the window is your most potent ad, but inform the hotels of your town or city, and its Chamber of Commerce, that your service is available. Keep them reminded. Have some printed cards that you can leave at hotel desks and see that there is always a supply of these cards there. Cultivate acquaintances of members of luncheon and other business clubs. They may need you at some time or may refer out-of-towners to you. You may have to work inconvenient hours at times, late at night or before 8 a.m., but regard this as an occupational hazard, a special accommodation that will increase the value of your service.

The Cash Flow:

Actual notarization is not lucrative, 25¢ per stamping. However, your charge for typing letters and documents may be at a relatively high rate, say $5 per page.

You have no rent, if you work at home, low rent if you prefer to arrange for desk space in an office suite. The project need involve no advertising expense except for the printed business cards.

RUBBER STAMPS

The Idea:

When you get a receipted bill marked PAID, someone has used a rubber stamp. There are rubber stamps by the hundreds, some standard, like AIR MAIL, and others special like those with a person's return address. They are used by businesses great and small, and also by individuals.

Rubber stamps are produced on a special machine, a small vulcanizing press, which takes little space—three or four square feet. The machine operates electrically with controlled heat of some 400°, with pressure of several hundred pounds per square inch. A type case holds the set type, the letters locked in place. Gum rubber is forced into a material called matrix. The result is a rubber stamp. You affix it to a mounting base and the stamp is ready for use. The current is that of an ordinary dwelling, no heavy current needed. Detailed instructions come with the machine.

Getting Started:

If you consider going into the rubber stamp business, to begin with you need mechanical aptitude. This sort of thing has been part of a man's world, but now, with women in the engineering classes in colleges, there are undoubtedly some who would quickly master this craft. You might be one of them. Next, the machine. The New York Yellow Pages, under Rubber Stamps - Mfrs.' Equip. & Supls., list three firms, and other major cities offer other names. It is best to get their literature and price to make your selection. Setting up the machine and learning to operate it will take some time, no matter how mechanically inclined you are, but once your confidence is established you are in business—or ready to be.

Try advertising in the Yellow Pages of your city's directory. Insert a small running ad in newspapers. Get some handbills printed and distribute them to businesses as widely as possible. Tell your friends who work in offices and show them some examples of your work. If you think it will promote good will and eventual business, give selected friends stamps with their names and addresses.

The Cash Flow:

The machine represents an initial investment of several hundred dollars. Probably you can work from home, in the basement or garage. You don't need much space but you do need a place to work hard and concentrate.

As for how much to charge per piece, at first, at least, you will do well to keep prices as low as you can, in the face of the competition you will undoubtedly have. Calculate all expenses, advertising, postage or other shipping, electricity, waste, etc.; estimate a gross profit; then try to establish a net of $10 an hour. In this calculation, you must include the time it takes you to make the stamp. After you are routined, you should be able to turn out a simple stamp in about ten minutes.

MENU TYPING

The Idea:

Many small and medium-sized restaurants offer their food through messy looking, processed menus. A good typist can bring her skill to the rescue here and enable a restaurant to present its offerings attractively. Exactly how? She can type the day's menus neatly, take the sheet to be Xeroxed, and hand immaculate, clearly legible copies to the restauranteur.

A housewife in the Midwest thought this one out, canvassed the eight restaurants in her town, and persuaded each to hand the job over to her.

Getting Started:

If this appeals to you and you set up a similar business of your own, you might study menus in the expensive restaurants and see what can be done on your typewriter to group the different dishes, ornament the groups, and emphasize the establishments' specialties. To avoid too much back and forth transportation, it might be well to use the typewriters of the different restaurants on your list, specifying that they must be kept in good condition. You can go to each restaurant at a different hour and thus service them all.

The Cash Flow:

Charges? Why not about $40 a week per restaurant, a

much lower cost to the clients than the salary of a full-time typist. It is probable that you can arrange a special price for volume copies with the firm owning the copy machine, since you will be coming daily and offering constant business to them.

TYPIST AT HOME

The Idea:

Are you an expert typist? Really expert? Can you type tables, chemical formulae, put material in ruled boxes, follow the correct style for footnotes and references? Can you arrange margins and spacing so that, if an author wants to add wordage after the page has been typed you can put in the extra line or two and still have a standard page?

If you set up as a free lance typist, working at home, your assignments will probably include term papers, theses and dissertations, as well as public documents and legal papers. All these have accepted forms, which it is important to follow, important to you, who want to do a satisfactory job and get further work, and to the author, since consideration by his readers depends a great deal on a presentation that is orderly, clearly documented, and free of mechanical errors. Novels and short stories are easier to type, but they, too, need to be set forth in clear, accurate typing, the dialogue correctly punctuated, with quotation marks and quote within quotes, commas in the right spot, margins even, and paragraphs uniformly indented.

Getting Started:

There are agencies that will secure such work for you and, since you must be expert and experienced before you begin to free lance in this way, you will have a former employer or employers who may be glad to pass on their overflow to you. Small ads in the business sections of newspapers are good, and notices on college bulletin boards often bring clients. And one happy client tells another, and so on.

There are books of reference you may want to read, perhaps own. "A Manual for Writers of Term Papers, Theses and Dissertations," by Kate L. Turabian, University of Chicago Press, is one. You need an excellent typewriter, of course, electric with all improvements. If you are fortunate enough to be able to type in more than one language, you should consult your typewriter dealer and find out what keyboard adjustments are necessary.

The Cash Flow:

If you don't have that fine, up-to-date typewriter, you will have to buy it. A portable is possible. One of the best of such free lance typists uses a Smith-Corona electric portable. Your advertising, if any, is another expense.

Your income will depend on the agency, if you have one. For work you get yourself, the price varies, from about 55¢ or 65¢ a page for straight typing to $2, $2.50, and even $3.50 a page for a very complicated assignment.

TEACH TYPING

The Idea:

Typing is more and more a required skill. Not only typists and stenographers need it but colleges want students to hand in themes and treatises typewritten; housewives need to write business letters and realize that they are much more effective when typed; orators save money by typing their own speeches, clergymen by typing their sermons; a member of a club can endear herself to all by typing minutes of meetings, letters, bills, and reports pertaining to the organization; even executives sometimes want to type an especially confidential memorandum or letter themselves.

Ability to type helps in many interesting jobs and activities by saving time and money. Some of the careers suggested in this book require typing, all are the better for it.

Ultra-modern techniques have brought a new advantage to the capable typist. The Compugraphic machines, direct-input photo typesetters, have a keyboard much like a typewriter, although with some sophisticated developments like 4-way keys. The makers claim that "just about any typist would feel right at home in front of the CompuWriter key-board." Some special instruction is neccesary, of course, in controlling the changing of type faces and sizes and other tricks the machine can perform, but the basic requisite is knowledge of standard typing.

An alert typist can cash in on all these needs for typing skill by holding classes in typing.

Getting Started:

You can start by teaching some of your friends. Then place an ad in newspapers offering instruction to paying students. Organize a typing curriculum, arranging the lessons so that students should be able to type reasonably well in twenty weeks. When your methods have proven themselves, mimeograph your own typing manual and sell it to students.

The Cash Flow:

Equipment consists of several rented typewriters and a generous supply of typing paper. A large room is needed, which must be rented if your own house does not offer proper space, and you need typing tables and chairs, which you can probably find in the second hand office furniture stores. You should start with a budget of approximately $500 for initial expenses and charge $50 to $75 for the course of twenty lessons. Your typing manual might be priced at $5.

12.

PROMOTION—
NO BUSINESS CAN
FLOURISH WITHOUT IT

PUBLIC RELATIONS

The Idea:

Public Relations is an elastic term, meaning a lot of things to a lot of people, but Webster's Seventh New Collegiate Dictionary defines it as "the art or science of developing reciprocal understanding and goodwill between a person, firm, or institution and the public; also: the degree of understanding and goodwill achieved." If you are in p.r., you can be working toward establishing goodwill and understanding in the interests of an individual, like an actor or singer; or for a business, big or little, General Motors or a small specialty shop; for a college or school; for a political figure who wants to be elected or reelected; for a government wishing to promote the products of its country; for a union seeking to build a benign image—the list could go on and on. The p.r. worker usually has background in some specialized field—theatrical, political, scholastic—or a commercial angle —automobiles, cosmetics, women's wear, publishing, oil—you name it.

How to build this understanding and goodwill? In general terms, if you are in p.r., you are like legal counsel, you tell the truth (if you are wise) but with emphasis on your client's virtues and usefulness. There are many media for underlining the good things about your client: newspapers, magazines, television and radio interviews; the giving of parties; willingness on your client's part to identify with constructive projects, to appear at philanthropic meetings and banquets to speak—and make a donation. The methods must fit the nature and individual needs of the person or organization, of course, but the idea is to show your client as sincerely carrying out a function that contributes to the community.

Getting Started:

If you want to go it on your own in this field, previous experience in a p.r. firm is a priceless asset, and so is a journalistic background. However, even if you have neither of these, ask yourself if you have the necessary attributes: ability to meet and like all sorts of people; to write a good, concise news release (if you can also write feature stories, that's fine, but the news release is a triple must); to answer questions promptly, tactfully—and truthfully; to organize gatherings, large and small; to keep your temper at all times.

This is a pretty good profession for the one-woman set-up, provided you can type and have an answering service to take care of calls while you are out. Mobility is very important and the best way to achieve it is to own and drive your own car.

To start, decide what your specialty is and try for some small accounts. If, for instance, you want to work in fashion, contact (first by letter and then in person) some manufacturers and shops near you. If you have worked for a p.r. firm, this is an excellent introduction. In any case, outline, in as attractive terms as possible, what you hope to do for them.

Public relations is a highly competitive field. In the New

York City Yellow Pages alone, there are seven full columns and two half-columns of the names of public relations counselors. These include the big ones and the little ones, the astronomically priced and the moderately priced. To succeed, you have to be good. But the fascination, and the (possible) rewards, are great.

The Cash Flow:

At first, at least, this business can be conducted from home. You need stationery, with the name, address, and telephone number of your service, and an answering service.

Strive to obtain your clients on a "retainer" basis, so much a month for a minimum number of months—say, six months. Fees vary from $200 a month to $1,000 a month depending on the volume of public relations you do and your expertise. As you achieve more clients and more public relations media contacts, your business can enjoy continued growth.

SELL ADVERTISING

The Idea:

Newspapers, as well as most other publications, are supported in large part by advertising. They are always looking for more of these revenue-bringing messages, from classified to full-page ads. Newspapers in the smaller centers, or neighborhood publications, often have editors who double as ad salesmen as well as writers. In many cases they welcome help in the selling end. If you believe you have talent as a salesperson in this field, why not try it?

Getting Started:

Your first sales assignment is to sell yourself to the editor or to the head of advertising, if these offices are divided between two people. Convince him (or her) that you understand the value to the client of representation in this medium and that you can convey the idea in such a way as to extract a commitment to take space. Then you go out and try your powers of persuasion on the prospects assigned you. These will probably be the smaller and more unimportant ones at first, the bigger and easier clients being jealously guarded by others on the sales staff, or possibly even by the head salesperson. You will probably have to prove yourself on small shops, restaurants and motels, on local teachers of music, secretarial skills, and so on, who have been holding out. This is the test.

If you do well, you will gradually get better opportunities. Perhaps you can build up a section, like the classified or the house for rent or sale.

The Cash Flow:

This work, as outlined, is a part-time, income supplementing occupation, at least at first. You certainly can work from home, and you learn as you go so there is no expense for schooling. To begin with, you will probably be on commission, and if so it ought to be a good one, say 25%. Later on, if you build up your following, a salary may be proposed, but by that time your income from commissions may be impressive enough for you to prefer to continue your original arrangement.

RESUMES FOR JOB APPLICANTS

The Idea:

An applicant for a job is usually asked to submit a type-written precis of his education and experience. A clear, comprehensive, easily read resume is worth a lot to a job seeker. Such a resume is good for general as well as particular use, can be multigraphed and sent to many companies, if an aspirant wants to cast his net widely. However, not everyone can write a good, effective resume, giving the most favorable picture possible of his qualifications.

Those who doubt their ability in this respect usually seek the help of someone who has made a study of resume-writing and gone into it professionally. Are you such a person, or would you like to be?

Getting Started:

If you want to write resumes as a paying proposition, your first requirement is an ability to present facts with emphasis on the most important and impressive. Get hold of as many resumes as possible and study them, for both do's and don't's. Textbooks on business procedures, available in the public library, will be of great help. Write a resume of your own experience and background and judge it as objectively as you can. Try writing some for your friends. Then if you are satisfied that you are good at this exacting type of writing, advertise in the classified sections, in the Yellow Pages, and through announcements on the bulletin boards of high schools and colleges.

After you get clients, you will find that, to prepare a resume you hold discussions to obtain information and learn qualifications, and if you are the kind of person who can send a client away from such an interview feeling encouraged and confident, this will be an intangible but valuable part of your service.

The Cash Flow:

This work can be done at home. The advertising budget is not large. However, you do invest considerable time and a specialized ability and the product is one of great value to the purchaser, so you are justified in charging $50 to $100 a resume. Clients will probably want you not only to write their original resume but to revise it periodically to keep it up to date and this should also entail a charge.

SALES LETTERS

The Idea:

Can you write a strong, convincing, persuasive sales letter? If so, you have a paying business right in hand. Almost all stores and other firms have occasion to send out regular sales letters to their customers and the composition of these letters is sometimes a great chore to the owner of the business or another executive.

A California woman realizes a good income by taking over the job of writing sales letters for several local firms. She was sparked off by reading the "junk mail" she received—philanthropic appeals, direct mail, and processed letters. This woman believed she could write better copy.

Getting Started:

She drew up a list of firms, including some she traded with, others culled from the telephone directory, telephoned for interviews, and went in with a portfolio of sample letters. In writing her letters she had a general plan: Imagine a typical customer; make the letter brief but tell the story; be conversational; and, above all, be sincere.

A number of her prospects were interested—and that was the beginning of a growing and successful business.

In servicing her customers, she not only writes the letters, she keeps in touch with developments of the firms, watches their advertising and literature, and works with any campaigns they put on. After a sales letter has been submitted to a client, and approved, either she or the firm has it multi-graphed or reproduced in another of the modern processes that make the copies look so amazingly like individually typed letters. If the firm does not have its own arrangements of this kind, finding the best and least expensive process is part of her service.

The Cash Flow:

Now the backbone of her business is the group of firms that pay her an annual retainer, instead of paying for each letter. She charges $25 and up for an individual letter, depending on its length. A retainer of $100 a month entitles a firm to four letters in that period.

Since this woman works from home, her expenses are light: telephone calls, carfare or the gasoline required to visit her clients, along with stationery and postage. She advertises in the local newspaper and Yellow Pages and sometimes conducts her own telephone campaign.

13.

SELLING— A ROAD TO THE BIG MONEY

LIFE INSURANCE AGENT

The Idea:

Life insurance, a very, very major business, and one of the most conservative, is now reaching out to draw women into its selling ranks. If you are considering the idea of selling life insurance, a pamphlet issued in the fall of 1975 by the Life Insurance Marketing and Research Association will encourage you. The pamphlet states that there are presently over fifty thousand women agents in this field and their number is increasing. A few years ago this was pretty much a business for males. Why is the welcome mat out for the qualified woman now?

For one thing, sex barriers are falling all over; for another, women have been proving themselves in the general sales field. A survey published in *Sales Management Magazine* and covering 161 sales executives, reveals that 71% of firms who employ women in the sales force want more. Reasons given: buyers will almost always see a woman representative, even if they have repeatedly refused to see a male representative from the same company; women representatives have proved highly memorable—prospective customers don't forget them; women tend to be better listeners than men and thus get a better idea of the prospect's needs; and finally, women, eager to prove themselves, may work harder than men.

So much for women's qualifications in the general sales field. Life insurance should perhaps appeal especially to women. The financial rewards can be dazzling, for one thing. As for job satisfaction, to quote Lee Rosler in his book, *Opportunities in Life Insurance Sales:* "What can be more satisfying than the knowledge that your work will provide economic security for widows and children and financial independence for persons facing retirement?" Life insurance companies invest in projects like low income housing, job training programs, the construction of hospitals, churches, schools.

Getting Started:

How does a woman latch on to a career in life insurance? To begin at the very beginning, whether you live in a metropolitan center or a small town, you undoubtedly know of an insurance office in your vicinity. Perhaps, even probably, you are insured yourself. First, talk to the local agents, or, by turning to the Yellow Pages, find the names of agents, regional offices, and CLU's (Certified Life Underwriters) and make an appointment.

Next, you should get an application blank from the company you wish to be identified with, and arrange an interview. At that time, the interviewer for the company will (1) size you up as far as possible and (2) give you as clear a picture as he or she can of the joys and sorrows ahead.

The next step is the training program of several weeks,

then a written examination, and then on-the-job training— after you pass the exam, you do actual selling, although you are still a trainee.

Cash Flow:

During this time—the training period, exam, and actual on-the-job training—you are on a salary.

This answers questions as to whether you need an initial investment to go into life insurance selling. No, you do not. This is one of the few businesses of its potential that does not require capital.

But, of course, after the salary stops a lean period may start.

Here's where you need those two great requisites of the successful life insurance agent: real liking for people and perseverance to go on in the face of—maybe—ten refusals in a row.

Once you've found your feet, the fascination grows. With experience, you sense the needs of clients, help them not only with straight life policies but with estate planning, annuities, health, and business insurance.

There is no limit to financial return. The amount of your commissions is governed by the number and value of the policies you place. It is not unusual, according to Bob Waldron, manager of press relations of the Institute of Life Insurance, for an agent, after five years or so of experience, to sell annually a million dollars worth of life insurance.

Wilhelmina Eaton of New York has passed the first hurdles and is off to a good start. She knows that, besides selling, she must continue the study programs that changing conditions make necessary, and she is willing to cancel a social weekend to call on prospects.

Advancement? Wilhelmina might, if she wishes, become a regional manager (although some of the agents under her would probably outearn her!). She can enter public relations like Bob Waldron, or go into statistical work like Edith Weiner, who—still in her twenties—is in charge of the Trend Analysis Program of the ILI. She can soar to the pinnacle of the business and become a CLU, like Mary E. Fort of Chevy Chase, Maryland, who, after some twenty years in life insurance, writes in *Sales Management Magazine:* "A sales person is a sales person, regardless of sex . . . . Women are endowed with the same ability as men when it comes to selling and require training that is no different from that given to men."

REAL ESTATE AGENT

The Idea:

Women have been on the real estate scene for a long time. That is, in the buying and selling of houses for family residences. Here, women have always been conceded a special flair. Only recently, however, have they been allowed to move into the commercial end, where office space is considered and chosen and buildings leased or bought for business purposes. There were no laws against women in commercial real estate, just one of those unwritten taboos.

Now women are beginning to move into this new activity, although many women prefer to stay in the residential part of the profession.

Real estate is a tough, challenging, highly competitive business, no place for sissies of either sex, but, for those who have the necessary qualities, it not only offers generous money returns, but holds a fascination that never fades.

Getting Started:

Real estate salespersons and brokers are licensed by the

different states. The specifics given here are for New York State but it may be assumed that the pattern is a general one. If you are interested in entering the real estate profession, you should write for information to the Department of State, Bureau of Licensing Services of your state.

Your first step is to get yourself identified with a licensed real estate broker. You receive a temporary license, rather like a temporary driver's license. As a beginner, you learn all you can from the broker, the other salespeople, and the appropriate literature. In a few weeks, the state will call you to take the examination for a Salesman's License, testing your knowledge of real estate terms and ethics and of the necessary math. This exam passed, your broker gets a copy of your Salesman's License and you receive a card for your wallet. You pay the fee, about $10.

How about money in the meantime? It's generally felt that you had better not start in real estate unless you can carry yourself financially for six months, at least. You are rarely on a salary. Your commissions are paid to your broker and you get half.

Experienced real estate agents feel that it takes about a year for a newcomer to learn the ropes, and that year may be hard going. It should get better as you go along. If you do not show promise after a reasonable time, you and your broker may have to part company. A new salesperson is an expense— desk space, telephone calls, advertising—and such expense must diminish by way of the business the newcomer brings in.

After two years as a licensed salesperson and after attending an accredited school, you are eligible to take the state examination for brokers. This brings you another license, certifying that you are a licensed real estate broker. The fee is about $50.

Now you can go it on your own, if you wish, open your own office and have your own sales staff.

It Can Be Done:

Peggy Carnegie of New York City has done all those things. Twenty years ago, Peggy was a housewife with a young daughter to support. Nine to five desk jobs had no appeal, so she looked in the Yellow Pages, chose Arthur Hardgrove, Inc., real estate broker, and went to see Malcolm Hardgrove, President. He gave her two weeks to make her first deal. Before the time was up, she had sold a seven-room co-op on Fifth Avenue.

Peggy, a broker since 1968, now has her own office and sales force. Recently she was elected a director of the Real Estate Board of New York (Brokerage Division), the first woman to be so honored in the board's seventy-nine-year history.

Peggy specializes in the sale of town houses and brownstones. She has put over some spectacular deals, including selling Audubon House on Fifth Avenue twice in one year.

She points out to neophytes and those eyeing the real estate field that you must pick your specialty. Present day real estate is too complex for anyone to divide time between residential and commercial selling and their phases. For example, do you want to work in a city, suburban, or rural setting? For residential selling, house, or co-op, or condominium, you need thorough knowledge of mortgaging, whereas for renting offices, you need to know leasing and price per square foot along with location, partitioning, etc. Then, there is land development, a specialty in itself—you envision the best place for residences, for grocery and other markets, for houses of worship, clubs, swimming pools. These are some of the specialties that are up for choice. But choose one, Ms. Carnegie advises. No one can do them all.

What are the prime requisites for a good real estate man or woman? Peggy says, first, physical stamina. In her specialty, town houses and brownstones, stair climbing is an absolute constant. The suburban real estate woman drives her car numberless hours a day. There is another, even more vital requirement—you must like people, all sorts and conditions of people.

If you can take the hours and the ups and downs, then real estate work can be not only financially rewarding, it can be the greatest fun.

MANUFACTURERS' REPRESENTATIVE

The Idea:

A manufacturers' representative is a salesperson in business for himself. He—or let's call this salesperson she—sells compatible, *not* competing products or services for one or more companies in a specified territory. She sells on commission. The advantage to the representative is independence, opportunity to build a high income, and the chance to choose the people she associates with. Manufacturers are likely to favor the representative system over maintaining their own sales staff because the former costs less and has proven efficient. Products sold by representatives are legion, including housewares, hardware, paint, chemicals, food processing equipment, cleaning services, mechanical supplies, you name it. Since none of the lines sold by a representative compete with each other, she can sell quantities of each to every customer visited. For instance, if you feature housewares, you can sell kitchenware, mops, brooms, and detergents, china, coffeemakers, a long list of related items, all (in theory, anyway) to the same store.

Getting Started:

This is no business for the inexperienced or untrained. Obviously, you need thorough knowledge of what you are selling, as well as how to sell. Representatives can come from sales management, purchasing, servicing, engineering. College graduates with special business management degrees are now entering the field. Personality traits needed are desire for independence; ability to sell and manage your own business; knowledge of a product, specific markets, or of a geographical territory, preferably all three; and strength, emotional and financial, to carry you through the first year or so. You must be free to travel—territories of representatives usually cover several states.

What are the first steps? You can probably work from home. Arrange for letterheads, envelopes, and business cards carrying the name of your agency—e.g., Jane Jones, Manufacturers' Representative—with address and phone number. Your telephone should be answered eight hours a day; if necessary get an answering service. Open a checking account. A lawyer and accountant are of the greatest help in setting up this (and any) business and will check on such matters as whether a license is required.

Your first lines may come from a previous employer or a friend who is a manufacturer. Check manufacturers' directories and write letters describing your background and service, contact marketing consultants, chambers of commerce, banks, trade shows, fraternal organizations, representatives' associations. You should have a continuing promotion program through direct mail and ads in publications. You need to reach two ways, to customers you sell to and to manufacturers you want to represent.

You make a separate contract with each manufacturer you represent. You and your lawyer should go over all contracts before you sign.

The Cash Flow:

The initial investment is modest: the price of stationery, telephone answering, perhaps some secretarial fees if you can't type yourself. But a car is a must in most territories, so add that expense. The big question is: Have you enough capital to provide for yourself and any dependents for at least a year before your agency begins to profit? Also, remember that this is a commission business, with no salary ever, so you will have good years and bad. You can also lose a client through no fault of your own, by a merger or changing sales policies.

Commissions vary widely, from 2% for high volume orders, to 25% and even 35% on items that take a long selling cycle. To check on the fairness of a commission, consult trade associations and other representatives.

DRESS SHOP AT HOME

The Idea:

If you are both fashion-oriented and in need of an interesting part-time occupation, one that can be operated from home, you might like to work with one of the many dress manufacturers. Fashion Frocks of Cincinnati, for instance, is one firm whose lines can be sold in your own house to your own friends. There are many such firms, producing garments covering a wide price range. Some arrange for you to hold a sales "party" in your living room, with a manufacturer's representative to take orders. The hostess, of course, gets a commission on each frock sold.

Other firms suggest a slightly different way of selling. One of these is Doncaster, a designer and manufacturer of Rutherfordton, North Carolina. Doncaster offers opportunity for you to sell their coats, dresses, suits, and evening wear, their Young Traditions line of separates and coordinates. The operation is all yours, with no representative there.

Getting Started:

The word is "never mind experience." In fact, if you have never sold before, this house believes your approach will be more versatile and imaginative than that of the career saleswoman.

The first step is to get in touch with the district manager for your part of the country for full information. A complete training course is given, with advice on fashion selling, and from there on you are free to develop your own ideas and style of presentation. Selling aids are provided, like an illustrated brochure that is also an invitation card, to be sent to prospective customers.

The individual touch is stressed in these garments, that is, each customer personally selects the style, color, and fabric of the dress or coat of her choice. There are special custom touches, like hand-sewn buttons, lace hem tapes, handtacked linings, lingerie straps, and generous seams. Prices are not low, but the manufacturer points out that, with the range of fabrics and colors to choose from, it is almost unheard of for a customer to see her dress on someone else.

The four showing seasons are fall, holiday and resort, spring, and summer. Number of showings each season is up to you.

The Cash Flow:

Your compensation is based on a percentage of what you sell, plus an opportunity for an annual bonus. You retain your own commission before sending in the balance of the suggested retail price. Based on average sales per saleswoman during 1975, Doncaster says a woman can expect to earn about $1,500. This represents taking an average from one woman who sold one dress and earned $25, to another who sold several hundred and earned over $10,000. Much depends on the clientele you can attract. The average amounts to about $400 a week for the time you are actually selling.

14.

LOVE ANIMALS?
YOU CAN MAKE IT PAY

DOG WALKER

The Idea:

A good, reliable dog walker is a welcome addition to almost any well-heeled neighborhood. By taking advantage of a dog walking service, owners who can pay the fee can escape the chore of taking the pet out on schedule in all weathers; or perhaps these owners are humane enough to want to ensure the walk when they themselves are kept at the office or are socially engaged.

If you wish to become a dog walker, people successful and experienced in that field will tell you that there is more to it than appears to the casual eye. To begin with, you should be thoroughly used to dogs, used to having them around, big, little, and middle-sized. Such an association will teach you that dogs are individuals, just as people are. Of course you should love dogs, but you should also be able to size up a subject's character and weaknesses. Dogs should trust you and, although you may not be able to return this trust whole-heartedly in all cases, you should be able to at least see a dog's point of view. Another requisite: You must be thoroughly reliable in the matter of turning up as agreed in regard to time and place. It is best to have someone who will act as back-up if you are sick or away.

Some dashing dog walkers take their canine clients in groups, strolling along the sidewalk, holding the leashes of perhaps half a dozen dogs of assorted sizes. The passerby wonders what would happen if misunderstandings and hostilities arise in the group. The answer is, of course, a disastrous riot. So better not attempt mass walking. Play it safe, take them one at a time, or never more than two big ones together, and limit the number of little dogs walked simul-taneously to four at the outside.

Patrecia Peil, head of Petti-Paws, Inc., who has operated this dog waking service on Manhattan's East Side for more than a decade, points out that, even if you have only one dog to walk, you can never take your mind off what you are doing, any more than if you have a child in tow. Some owners, taking out their own dogs, permit their pets to to approach and sniff at strange dogs. This can lead to a dog brawl—and to bites. Also, the dog in your charge just *could* get run over if you are careless crossing streets. Mrs. Peil, whose business long ago grew so extensive that she had to hire a staff, never accepts an applicant dog walker under twenty-five. This time of life, while beyond the age of consent, is, in her opinion, the beginning of the age of responsibility. Mrs. Peil has found that no insurance is available to a dog walker as such, although she and her staff are bonded, since they must sometimes enter houses and apartments to pick up and return dogs in the absence of the owner.

Getting Started:

If you have the qualifications of a dog walker and want to start on your own, a good way to get customers is to become friendly with as many vets as possible and with owners of pet-grooming establishments. Ask them to let you leave some printed cards on their premises announcing your services and request them to mention your name to owners who might be interested. An ad in the Yellow Pages is usual in this work. Also, small ads in neighborhood publications can be productive of new patrons.

Go into a huddle with your lawyer and find out about any license necessary. As time goes on, you will find out other requirements, such as checking to see if a dog you are about to walk has a rabies tag on his collar. If not, you may get in trouble with the law, whether you are the owner or not.

The Cash Flow:

Since at times you will be entering or leaving a home or apartment when the owner is out, bonding must be considered. The cost of your printed cards and of an ad in the Yellow Pages is not excessive. As for fees, charges of dog walkers vary a great deal, but if you know dogs, can be depended on to keep your engagements, and provide experienced help that is valuable to your customers, you are justified in asking a high price.

HELP LOCATE LOST DOGS

The Idea:

The owner of a dog that has been lost or stolen is usually a person badly in need of help and counsel.

A woman in New England, herself a devoted dog fancier, has a service for such bereaved owners. She watches the lost and found columns for the distress signals, contacts the owners and offers to include a description of the lost dog and the name and address of the owner in a multigraphed circular that she sends regularly to all the pet shops in the vicinity.

These descriptions alert the pet shop in case a stolen dog is brought in for sale.

Numerous owners have been glad to pay for the insertion of the notice, and the circular has been the happy means of restoring a number of dogs to their homes, besides realizing a profit for the instigator of this service.

Getting Started:

If you want to carry on such an activity, the first thing to do is to subscribe to all the newspapers of your section so as to keep up with the ads for the lost pets; the second is to scan the Yellow Pages of the telephone books of your city and the neighboring centers for the names of pet shops. All pet shops must be on your mailing list or your delivery route to receive your circular, and to receive it free of charge. Also, you would be wise to go and see the owners of pet shops, or write each a letter, telling of your forthcoming circular and its use, so that they do not think it is just junk mail and throw it away without reading it.

Next you contact multigraphers and discuss your project and get their prices. Low price is a good thing but it must go with prompt service. Your circular should come out on time and be received with regularity, by the pet shops and by the dog owners as well, so that they can see the notice they are paying for.

The final step is to contact the distressed owners and offer to help them by publicizing their loss in the proper quarters. When you begin to bring about successful reunions, ask the fortunate owners to write you letters acknowledging the effectiveness of your circular. Multigraph these letters and use them for mailing pieces.

The Cash Flow:

Multigraphing, postage, and the subscriptions to newspapers are your primary expenses, all continuing expenses. Your income is the fee for the inclusion of the description of the lost pets. This cannot be low, and should be $35 for one insertion, $50 for two, $75 for a description run three times.

LIVE-IN PET SITTER

The Idea:

A New York woman lives in luxury a good part of her time by acting as a live-in sitter for pets of the rich whose owners have gone to Florida, are off on a cruise, or have been called away for some other reason. Such owners are often too concerned with their pets' happiness to think of placing the canine or feline member of the family in a kennel or pet boarding establishment. Cats, especially, are high strung creatures and dislike change of environment. The animal kingdom of a client may not consist of dogs and/or cats; there may be an aquarium of rare tropical fish, a cherished parakeet, parrot, canary, or some more exotic bird.

The pet sitter sometimes has a staff of servants to look after the house and cook and serve the meals, but she still has her work cut out for her. There is generally quite a regime. Dogs must be walked, fed (and sometimes the daily menu is varied and demanding), watered, bathed, and kept from being bored. Cats are easier, except for occasional dietary eccentricities. Fish must be fed at the correct times and the water in the tank changed and maintained at the right temperature. Birds' cages need frequent cleaning and they must have the *right* seed or whatever, and fresh water.

One single household is not likely to have all these pets, but there often are several dogs of assorted breeds and sizes, or a dog and cat that may or may not have to be kept separated. Even one pet, if spoiled, can be demanding and difficult, especially a dog who misses the owner and falls into a melancholy.

Getting Started:

This is a hard project to get started unless you know someone from the upper income brackets who needs such services and knows that you are the one to fill the post. If you successfully carry out one such job, it is probable others will follow through good old word-of-mouth recommendation.

If you don't know an initial client, you might go around to pet shops in exclusive neighborhoods and leave some printed cards and mimeographed literature describing your qualifications. Drive out in the country and talk to owners of kennels and ask if you can leave your literature. If your town or city has a neighborhood paper of magazine reaching the high income district, take an ad in that. Getting started is the problem. After a few successes, it should be easier.

The Cash Flow:

Expenses range from nothing to a modest advertising budget for the printed cards and mimeographing, and any small ads. As in the case of the dog walker, you should be bonded, since you are living in someone else's house or apartment in the absence of the owner.

Charges have to be carefully considered. Well-heeled people often hate to pay out and are inclined to count the live-in part as reward enough. However, you not only live-in in this job, you work. So charge, perhaps $50 a day.

ANIMAL CEMETERY

The Idea:

In the suburbs of New York are some half-dozen cemeteries devoted to the burial or cremation of pets. An ad for one offers complete funeral services "at our beautiful chapel," another stresses understanding (presumably for the bereaved owners) and a service, still another cites knowledge, dignity, and understanding "in a most appropriate tribute." Perhaps the oldest of these cemeteries, one that will inter all pets, including birds, has been operating since 1896.

Undoubtedly such cemeteries do represent a service, more to animal loving humans than to the pets themselves. Grieving owners, from juveniles to octogenarians, may feel the need for one last tribute to beloved Shep, or Ginger, or Charlie the Songster.

Equipment for the cremation of pets may be priced beyond the normal budget, but if owners are satisfied with burial, perhaps operation of an animal cemetery might not be beyond the reach of someone looking for a self-employed project.

Getting Started:

The location would be the first problem; anyone interested should consult a lawyer in regard to possible licensing and zoning and health laws. Perhaps a rural spot, not too far from town and with access to the highway would be best. If you know someone who has made an unfortunate investment in a sufficiently isolated lot, perhaps this investor might lease you the ground or sell at a reduced rate.

Animal cemeteries provide transportation for the deceased. For this, a station wagon should suffice, even if the departed is a St. Bernard, although a horse would present a problem. Larger animals are excluded.

If the mourners wish to hold a funeral service and attend the burial, they should provide their own transportation. Probably they will want to write their own words of farewell, but you should have a funeral service mimeographed and ready to offer if it is desired. The grave should be dug ahead of time.

The Cash Flow:

Unless you are lucky enough to own a suitable piece of ground, your lease or payments loom large in your budget. Advertising can be confined to the Yellow Pages and word will get around among pet owners. Have a sign designed and painted to mark the entrance to the cemetery. The field or lot should be fenced, if it is not already so enclosed, and this fence must be kept in good repair, which will be a continuing expense. If you are sturdy enough to dig the graves yourself, this is a saving. You can drive the station wagon-hearse yourself with a back-up driver available if you are sick or away.

Charges can be high—say, $200 and up, with care of the grave included. If there is a monument, you should get a commission from the supplier. Also, some sort of wooden box or coffin must be offered, priced around $15 for the small ones (for birds, hamsters, etc.), to $50 for the larger ones.

PLANT SITTER

The Idea:

City and country dwellers alike are fond of bringing the outdoors indoors by growing house plants. Once started, the craving increases, beginning perhaps with a simple philodendron and progressing to ivy, begonias, African violets, and then rubber plants (trees, really). People take seeds of avocados, plant them, and watch fascinated as they sprout and flourish.

All this is wonderful as long as the grower stays on hand to prune and water the plants, especially water. But as time passes, the grower wants to go on vacation, is called away on business, must go to a distant city to visit a sick relative.

Is this indoor garden, gathered lovingly and cherished warmly, to be allowed to perish? Not necessarily. Here's a chance for someone to provide a useful service and one not too often met with. This someone can watch and water plants while the fond owners are absent. Those who engage in it have found this to be a profitable part-time business.

Getting Started:

Such a project does not call for any highly specialized training, but the more you know about house plants, the better you can operate. Some plants need lots of water; others, like the cacti, can be destroyed by too much soaking. Some plants need special foods and fertilizers, others need different temperatures at different stages of growth. Clients do not always leave adequate instructions, believing that they are justified in expecting the plant sitter to know the proper course to follow. If you are in doubt as to what to do for the best in the care of a certain plant, better telephone the nearest botanical garden and ask for expert advice.

Reliability on your part is vital. If you promise to come in and look after the plants twice a week, or whatever schedule is agreed on, you must do just that without fail. If you are ill or unavoidably absent, you should have a back-up to carry out the assignment.

Ads in local and neighborhood papers can inform prospective clients of your service, and a short, recurring ad on the radio might help. One plant fancier will tell another about you, and this kind of commendation may well be your best publicity.

The Cash Flow:

Since the life of the plants is in your hands, owners should be willing to pay. Fees might be set by the week, say $25; or $15 for a single visit.

Your expenses will be advertising, plus the gas for your

car when you go on your rounds. Oh, yes, you should be bonded, since you enter dwellings in the absence of the householder.

15.

IF YOU LIKE PEOPLE, SINGLY, OR IN THE AGGREGATE

BOWLING CENTER

The Idea:

Bowling seems one sport that the great American public never tires of. Its patrons range widely in age, income, and occupation. Judges like to bowl as much as chefs, fashion models keep their figures by bowling, and researchers for scientific labs get away from the test tubes and retorts by visiting the alleys.

So, if you can get a location in a populous zone and not too near an established competitor, starting a bowling center can be good business.

Four types of bowling games are played in the United States: tenpin bowling, which accounts for about 95% of the play throughout the country; and three games with smaller balls and pins—duckpin, rubberband duckpin, and candlepin bowling. Duckpin bowling is played in New England and the

Middle Atlantic states, rubberband bowling in the Pittsburgh area, and candlepin bowling in New England, especially Massachusetts. So the chances are you will choose tenpin bowling. All types use standard specification lanes.

Getting Started:

You should be familiar with all aspects of the operation, and the best way to acquire such knowledge is to work for a bowling center for a year or so. You should get in touch with the trade associations and manufacturers of bowling equipment and learn what they offer in training and guidance. You need to develop skill in business management in general, merchandising, promotion and advertising, personnel management, keeping financial records. You also have to have that practically unversal requirement for success in business, a liking for people and ability to get along with them. You and your employees must provide a clean, relaxed, pleasant environment.

Organizing ability is another quality you will find invaluable. You must arrange schedules and see to it that your employees adhere to them without creating ill will. Your main source of business will be bowling leagues and it is, therefore, a public relations necessity to offer pleasant and smooth service that will bring them back year after year.

The Cash Flow:

This business calls for a large investment to begin with. Bowling equipment is expensive and operating costs are not low. Equipment (automatic machines) can be leased, but, as with purchased equipment, the cost of installation is considerable. Manufacturers of such bowling equipment help with financing, but they generally require a substantial down payment. They also offer help in general planning, in choosing location, training employees, and so on.

Usually 70% to 80% of your total income will be from the

game itself, but many centers get extra income from snack bars, fountain service, vending machines, bars and lounges, locker rentals, shoe rentals, pro shop sales, amusement devices. These sidelines can be concessions run by outsiders or can be managed by the center's owner.

Profit surveys are made from time to time. One in 1963, embracing 354 bowling centers, found that 179 made no profit. However, owners' salaries, comprising 9.3% were included in expenses. The typical firm showing a profit listed owners' salaries as 7.3%, with net profit of 5.3%. Typical annual sales ranged from $82,000 for 12-lane alleys to more than $300,000 for 32-lane establishments.

WAKE-UP SERVICE

The Idea:

If you're the type that functions only after three cups of coffee and the stroke of twelve noon, don't read this. But if you like rising early, why not consider a Wake-Up Service for a business? There are plenty of reluctant risers in any town or city who need more than an alarm or clock radio to really get them going. It has been found that such sleep-lovers respond to a summons, first by the telephone's ring, and then by a pleasant human voice.

Getting Started:

Customers can be attracted through small newspaper ads and through referrals. As the business builds up, try short radio commercials on the local station. Radio time is sold in 10-, 30-, and 60-second spots. Use a short, pithy approach and see what you can do with 10 seconds. Like: *"Alarm sounds. Voice:* Attention, sleepy-heads! Need a wake-up service? Call (give telephone number)."

This service is home-based and all you need is a telephone

to make calls and receive bookings. Main initial investment: a telephone answering service or machine to take messages when you are out.

The Cash Flow:

Your expenses are your telephone bill and advertising budget. If you charge $5 a month in a fair-sized city, you can hope to build up to, say, 150 customers, with a gross of $750.

Working hours are usually confined to the early morning, leaving the rest of the day for promotion of the project—or even for another job.

BRIDGE LESSONS

The Idea:

Pity the poor mediocre bridge player surrounded by real aficionados of the game. There are many of these pathetic hangers-on, sometimes married to spouses who are sharks. If you are (a) a fine bridge player, (b) one who can be patient and encouraging to a slow learner, then you might find your ideal pastime-that-brings-money by giving bridge lessons. Surely you would be justified in having pupils pay well for the satisfaction of astonishing their former critics.

Getting Started:

Giving bridge lessons will probably start as a part-time occupation and can be offered at home. Equipment—several decks of cards, score pads, a bridge table and chairs.

Ideally, you should take three students at a time, but when this is not practical, you can play with open hands. Suggest books on bridge for outside reading and point out some of the excellent bridge columns in the newspapers. Encourage your pupils to play as much as they can. Many a middling player has improved and conspicuously raised his level of play just by faithfully keeping at the game. And many a potentially good player has remained in beginner status because he doesn't bother to play often.

When you get enough pupils to have several sessions at different hours, give an occasional general session, with interchange of partners.

Serving tea, cookies, and interesting little snacks cuts profits, but makes up for it in goodwill.

The Cash Flow:

This project probably can be carried on without much advertising. One student will tell another of your sessions, saying, you hope, that besides being highly instructive, they are good fun. And when your much-improved star pupils begin ranking high in the Women's Club Annual Tournament, your fame will really begin to snowball.

A small running ad in your newspaper is good, however, if only to keep your name before the eyes of the editor, who may give you an occasional mention, item, or even story in the columns.

If you do this from home, your expenses are low. Charges should be made for a course of twenty lessons, scheduled as two hours of play, perhaps twice a week, and might run to $100. This would break down to $5 per lesson, per player; if you had at least three pupils at a time, to $15 for two hours work for yourself, or $300 for the course.

RECORD STORE

The Idea:

If you are a music buff, love music in all its phases, classical and pop, and have some background of musical education, then you might have a yearning to open a record store.

Before you take this step, take stock of your practical knowledge of such operation. You need to know not only music, but the latest developments in stereo and hi-fidelity. You should be able to judge customers' tastes. Besides this, you need to be familiar with management practices, such as bookkeeping, personnel, and arrangement and display on the floor and in the window. Another must is knowledge of your sources of supply, especially availability of franchised lines, along with inventory control.

How do you acquire all this know-how? The best way is to get a job in a record shop and earn and learn.

Getting Started:

When you have had an employee-eye view of the record business, you will be in a much better position to determine whether you really do want to open your own store. If you do, and have or can borrow sufficient funds to begin (see Chapter II), then one of the first things to consider is location. If your stock is principally phonograph records, try to locate in a shopping area or near a school, but watch out for competition from department stores and general retailers nearby.

Record manufacturers will help you in selection of equipment, floor lay-out and merchandising methods. Attractive and convenient arrangement of the records is very important, especially if you have self-service. There should be room for customers to stand and examine records at leisure and there should be an adequate number of listening booths, as well as listening posts with earphones.

The broader your musical knowledge, the more ably you can discuss tonal trends with your customers and the more they will respect you. Keep up with music news. Read the trade journals, like *Billboard* and *Record World*.

The Cash Flow:

The amount of capital you need at first will be governed by the lines and volume of inventory to be carried. It would seem advisable in most cases to start with a limited, carefully selected stock. Later, as you are better acquainted with local taste, you can expand the appropriate categories of records.

To make sure of a profit, you have the job of remembering that you are both an art center and a business. Encourage record clubs and evening record concerts, pop and classical. Display posters for coming live music events. Love of live music will send customers to your store to obtain the means of living over moments of musical pleasure.

DEMONSTRATOR

The Idea:

Can you meet people well, grasp and convey information quickly, think on your feet? Can you take a table and a few samples of a product, some literature and a poster or two and make an attractive display? Then you probably would make a good demonstrator of food, cosmetics, household appliances, or the like.

This is a fairly demanding work, needs physical stamina (you stand for hours) and the ability to speak well and also to listen. For the right person, it offers interest, variety and, probably, relatively constant employment.

In this activity you do not need any long training. You will be briefed on the product, asked to read the literature and to convey the impression that you believe what you are saying. Insincerity is as apparent here as anywhere.

When you are engaged to demonstrate a product, it is a good idea to go ahead of time and survey the space you will occupy, then on demonstration day arrive early and set it up effectively. No longer is a demonstrator expected to make a "spiel" like a carnival barker. You greet passers-by and play the gracious hostess, offering samples and showing interest in their reactions and making sure that people take the literature.

Getting Started:

If you think you would be a good demonstrator, how do you start? If you live in a large city, you contact public relations and marketing firms and let them know you are available for showing their clients' wares. In both big and little cities you contact the department stores and offer to set up demonstrations for special occasions or to introduce new products.

The Cash Flow:

The pay here might vary, depending on the size of the store and city and the local wage scale. Perhaps $5 an hour for a ten to four o'clock day, excluding lunch hour; or $50 a day, flat rate, if that amount seems possible for the section and the business employing you. Employment can be reasonably steady if you earn the name of a successful demonstrator and keep your clients reminded of your availability.

Expenses are low, no office rent or media advertising. Perhaps you need an answering service for when you are away from your home telephone, and a letter campaign to local merchants and firms may help, but mostly yours is a face-to-face business, with engagement leading to engagement.

DAY CAMP

The Idea:

A large cabin or lodge, on or near a lake, can yield summer dividends as a day camp for vacationing children.

Perhaps the lodge is your own that you've owned while your children were growing up; or it might belong to a neighbor whose offspring are post-teen-age and off on their own. The latter lodge may be a bargain to buy or rent.

A day camp can be fun, if you love and are used to working with the young. But it's a big responsibility, children at play, especially in the water. If you have not had thorough camp counselor experience yourself, better—*much* better—hire a reliable swimming instructor and lifeguard. There are many things to do besides swimming, of course: crafts, all kinds of games involving balls, cook-outs, station wagon trips to nearby sights or historic spots and, for the hardier campers, survival training.

Getting Started:

Assuming you have the proper building and location, the next thing is to decide how many campers you can handle. Then assemble a list of parents to be contacted, socially (your personal friends) or by telephone or mail. Those lists are of the first importance and should be kept scrupulously up-to-date in a card file, with notes added from time to time. You can, of course, advertise in the local media, but you will probably find that contact through your precious mailing lists, along with recommendations from parents whose children have been your campers, is the best way of attracting new children to replace the ones who outgrow your camp or move away.

The Cash Flow:

In computing your charges, remember that your running expenses include at least one meal a day and probably a snack as well, time devoted to marketing, and garbage disposal. Unless you have a mini-bus, it will probably be necessary to specify that transportation is the responsibility of the parents. Certainly, before opening this project, you must discuss it with your insurance agent and be properly covered. There is also upkeep of the buildings. A day camp is a summer project, but there will be promotion work in the winter, using those valuable lists.

To calculate all expenses as adequately as possible will be a task, but a necessary one, even if you have to call in your accountant. When it is worked out, try to obtain some 50% profit per camper.

PLAY SCHOOL

The Idea:

In the world of the '70's, most mothers have jobs, in offices, in their own businesses, in community projects. What to do with the pre-schoolers?

If you have a love for and affinity with small children, you might find a congenial occupation, with financial opportunity, in opening a play school.

Getting Started:

Before deciding on this activity, try to visit as many play schools as you can. If you live in a city, there undoubtedly are some not too far from you. If you live in a rural district where there are no such schools within convenient driving range, then get as much literature on the subject as possible from a public library. If the library does not have a book that you want, they can secure it for a limited period from a larger library.

Are you going to devote part of your own house to the school? If so, you need a colorful, eye-catching sign on the front lawn. Also, whether you are starting this project at home or in some rental property, it is vital that you consult your lawyer and make sure you conform to your state's health and fire laws and your city or town's zoning laws. You should also find out what insurance is necessary.

How about transportation? Will you require the parents to bring and call for their offspring, or can you get a mini-bus and pick them up?

From reading and observation, you can draw up a possible program of creative play and, of course, the menu for a meal or snack, depending on the length of time you mean to give the children each day. There are plenty of things to do, paper work, coloring, cut-outs, elementary singing and dancing, the beginning of music appreciation.

The Cash Flow:

You need a lot of toys. These might be bought second hand from a neighbor, toys made obsolete by the young owner outgrowing or getting tired of them. You also need tables and chairs, child size, a blackboard, visual aids, a record player. The food for the snack is a constant in your budget.

You might order colorful stationery, perhaps with an imprint of the sliding board in your front yard, or the see-saw with two youthful figures on it. Try direct mail on such stationery. Get a list of families with children the right age and write to them in a friendly, informal style. Ads help, in local newspapers, on radio and, if possible, local television. Along with such a campaign, try for feature stories in your press and other media. If you get a good newspaper story, with pictures, have it multigraphed and use it as a mailing piece.

All this brings up the cost of operation, especially if you rent. Charges should be by the month or the term and should be calculated (you may have to call in your accountant here) so as to give you a profit of at least 40%.

AFTER-SCHOOL-HOURS CARE

The Idea:

During the months when school is in session many

children whose mothers work are unsupervised after school. How about a place for some of them to go? Working mothers will probably be glad to pay for being freed from a constant anxiety.

If you like this idea, you don't need a degree or even special experience to start such a service, but you do need to know children, your own or some other children who have been close to you, to know how to keep them occupied and happy, to distract them from anything dangerous or unwholesome, to maintain the peace when a hostile youngster starts throwing his weight around. Also, how many children can you take on? Six? Four? Ten? What ages? Do you prefer them all eight to eleven, or would you accept a wider age range, with the big ones sharing the responsibility for the smaller ones?

What space in your house can you offer the children? Have you, for instance, a large family room in the basement? What activities will you suggest, games, nature walks, hikes? In bad weather, perhaps television watching, a drama club, table games, story hours, corn popping?

Getting Started:

When you have settled all these questions in your mind, perhaps the most effective method of publicizing is to tell everyone you know about your project. Ask young mothers to pass the word along in their offices, put notices on as many office bulletin boards as possible. If you belong to the PTA, or if your friends do, circulate the rumor there of after-school-care and confirm it to all inquirers.

After you have, through these methods, assembled a little band of juveniles and establish that you give them good care, along with interesting supervised play, these children themselves will be your best publicity agents by giving a good report to pals and parents. Probable result: a waiting list for your service.

In this activity, as in any project involving children, be sure to consult your lawyer about the fire, zoning, and sanitary laws of your state and locality.

The Cash Flow:

Since you probably operate from home, you have no rent. However, children are usually ravenously hungry after school, so something like a milk and cookie snack is pretty essential, adding both to the general joy and to the expenses. You should make it plain that you do not provide transportation. Children can probably come in groups from school and either go home by themselves or be picked up by parents. This makes it advisable for at least most of your children to live nearby.

Your fees should probably include after-school care for a school term, beginning of school to Christmas vacation, then first of the year to end of school term. A suggested fee might be $10 to $15 a week per child per term.

LONG-TERM CHILDREN SITTERS

The Idea:

A flourishing business has been established by a woman in an industrial city: a bureau supplying long-term children sitters. Many men and women of her locality have to travel on business, to Europe, Latin America, or some distant part of their own country. These people are parents in many cases and the problem arises, what to do about the children?

The solution for a large number of them has been supplied by the woman mentioned in the first sentence. She canvassed her neighborhood, the nearby senior citizen centers and churches, and assembled a group of women who are available to stay in a house and take over the role of "live-in" sitter for periods of from one to three weeks.

Getting Started:

Among her own acquaintances were several of the men and women who needed her service—couples where the wife works, divorced men with children, couples wanting to take a vacation trip. She tried out her idea with them, found it worked well, and then decided to go into it in a bigger way. She advertised in newspapers, in Yellow Pages, and on local radio, and relied on people telling each other of her service.

This woman operates from home, her chief equipment being a filing cabinet for the names and telephone numbers of her sitters.

The Cash Flow:

Her expenses are low, since she pays no rent, and consist in great part of her telephone bill and the cost of an answering service. She charges $200 a week to her clients and pays the sitters $125.

PART-TIME CHAUFFEURS

The Idea:

There are many occasions when the family car is available but not the family driver. Trips to and from the airport, shopping trips, transporting an aging relative to and from regular visits to the doctor—anyone can name dozens of such legitimate needs for a car, with no driver around.

When you see a need, if you can fill it, you've got a business. A New England woman has done just that with the part-time chauffeur demand. She has a file of fifty drivers, some of whom are on call twenty-four hours a day. They use the customers' cars and drive them wherever they wish to go.

Getting Started:

In such a business, you can work from home because all

you need is a list of reliable drivers and some file drawers for their names and addresses, plus a telephone and an answering service. The drivers can be housewives, moonlighting school teachers, college men and women on vacation or in their off hours, anyone who wants to supplement their income and has free hours at regular intervals—along with a driver's license and an unblemished traffic record.

The Cash Flow:

The overhead is small since you operate from home with your clients' cars. Pay the drivers four dollars an hour and charge the customers from seven to eight dollars. This leaves you a nice net, spreads joy among the drivers, and encourages clients to become repeaters.

AUTOMATIC CARWASH

The Idea:

If you aspire to establish yourself as owner of an automatic carwash, you probably would be among the charter members of women in such occupations. No statistics are available at the moment, but undoubtedly the number of female owners in the field is small. So, if you want to be a pioneer and a groundbreaker, here is a chance.

Getting Started:

According to a counseling note of the Government's Small Business Administration, better not undertake keeping your neighbor's cars clean unless you have specific training in equipment maintenance and operating procedures, are good at planning, have management ability, imagination, determination, and the ability to work hard. Tact and patience help, too.

If you have all that, and can draw customers from a

population of at least 25,000, can command the necessary cash outlay, you still need a special location, in an area convenient to the necessary population, near a main artery of traffic, with easy entrances and exits. Be sure to check zoning laws—they could be a problem.

Your first outlay for plant and property for a full-size conveyor-type carwash is about one-quarter to one-third of the total price for a down payment. Your building should be in the center of the lot to allow for cars to drive around the building and park for drying and vacuuming. Before locating, be sure to select a site where all utilities, such as sewers, water lines and electricity are already in. The expense of any of these could stop your whole project.

There is a trade association you can join, Automatic Car Wash Association International, 4415 West Harrison Street, Hillside, Illinois 60162, and several trade publications. The Small Busines Administration can give you helpful advice here, as in so many other phases of the work.

The Cash Flow:

Considerable capital is necessary to start. For a conveyorized automatic carwash, some $150,000 to $200,000 is necessary, between $50,000 and $70,000 going for car washing equipment, the balance toward the building and factors like utilities installation, paving, and signs. There are new types of exterior carwashes that can be built for around three-quarters of the price of the fully-conveyorized model. Other semi-automatic and wand-type units cost from $50,000 to $100,000. Your supplier may assist you by giving you a break in credit. Also, there are a few franchisers who offer help in getting established.

Let us say your plant turns out 25,000 to 75,000 cars a year, with a net income of 5% to 8% of dollar volume, this percentage including both your salary and interest on your investment.

16.

SUCCESS CASE HISTORIES

MADELINE McWHINNEY
SHE PIONEERS AS A WOMAN BANK PRESIDENT

The marquee of one of the most prestigious buildings on New York's East 57th Street carries the large lettering, "The First Women's Bank." The first, second, and last words are black, the third word red, from which you deduce that the operative word is "Women's."

When you go inside and check on personnel, visible and invisible, as well as on depositors, you begin to realize that, in the language of relativity, this is both true and untrue.

True because, as Madeline McWhinney, the bank's tall, personable president, will tell you, the bank was created to be a sort of showcase for women's abilities in banking.

Untrue because, as she will continue, this bank, recently chartered, is dedicated to a strictly non-discriminatory policy, such policy including, of course, equal opportunity for men.

The First Women's Bank came into being because it was apparent that, for a while, anyway, banks were not putting women in senior spots. Law suits to right this situation were filed under the FEPC. However, a pleasanter way to accomplish the same end was to establish a special bank, one that would give opportunity to women and prove by actual example their competence as bankers.

Two of the moving spirits in forming such a bank were Carol Greitzer, New York City Councilwoman, and Eileen Preiss, former Vice-Chairperson, N.Y. State Democratic Committee. While the bank was being organized, it was not easy to find women to fill the top posts because there actually were few women who had been given the requisite experience. The two senior loan officers *had* to be men, although this caused no grief—it was in line with the nondiscriminatory policy.

The name "The First Women's Bank" was chosen because the basic purpose was to assist women in all sorts of business, and the bank has been instrumental in launching women in such varied fields as publishing, cosmetics, office supplies, and importing. But the loans have been by no means confined to women. In fact, Ms. McWhinney believes that in five years time the word "Women's" in the title will have no more significance to the public than the word "Seamen's" in the Seamen's Bank for Savings. She points out that the Bank of America was originally "The Bank of Italy," its early purpose to assist Italian-American truck farmers.

Madeline McWhinney joined the group organizing The First Women's Bank in January, 1974, as its first president—a logical choice for this vital spot. Her qualifications for the job are dazzling. Primarily she had been with the Federal Reserve Bank of New York and was its first woman officer. She was responsible for the development and management of a large computer center specializing in statistical processing and economic analyses for the Research and Statistics Foundation of the Reserve Bank; served as chairperson of the System Committee responsible for the administration of all the Reserve System's current statistical programs; was a member of the committee which designed and installed the Reserve System's electronic funds transfer system, and of the Long Range Planning Committee. She was on the Boards of Directors of the Retirement System of the Federal Reserve Bank and the American Finance Association; president of both the Money Marketeers (an association of bankers and brokers) and the Downtown Economists Luncheon Group.

Ms. McWhinney's current affiliations include membership on the Boards of Trustees of the Carnegie Foundation of New York, The Charles F. Kettering Foundation, the Board of Advisors of the Education Foundation of the National Association of Bank Women, and the Board of Directors of the Investor Responsibility Research Center, Inc.

Ms. McWhinney is a second-generation bank president; her father, Leroy McWhinney, a lawyer, was head of the International Trust Company of Denver, her birthplace. The young Madeline enjoyed Sunday walks with her father, who would sometimes talk to her of the joys and sorrows of banking. She was Phi Beta Kappa at Smith and later received an MBA in finance from New York University's Graduate School of Business. She has since received N.Y.U.'s Meritorious Service Award and the Smith Medal.

In 1961, she married Dr. John D. Dale, president of Dale Elliott & Company, Management Consultants. They have one son, Thomas D. Dale. The family lives on a six-acre estate on the New Jersey shore, and also have a Manhattan apartment. Family hobbies are cooking and gardening, and Thomas and his mother play tennis together.

Madeline McWhinney sees a bright future for women in banking. "The pipelines are open now," she says, "and banks are beginning to look on promising employees as bright 'people,' regardless of sex—and that is what sex equality is all about."

STELLA DRATLER
SHE MADE IT IN FOOD

Stella Dratler's advice to a woman starting her own business is exactly the same as she would give a man in the same situation.

Ms. Dratler, who has been on the advertising and publishing scene since 1948, for the most part on her own, thinks if you—and let's say you are a woman—are contemplating a solo flight into the wild blue yonder of business, you should first consider finance, assuming, of course, that you have already selected a pursuit you like and are suited to. A sound financial basis is essential, and this means, to begin with, that you have some money saved up, or perhaps an inheritance, or a spouse who is making enough to pay the home rent and grocery bills until your business begins to pay, and also to cover the initial expenses of setting up the business. These may be relatively heavy, as in opening a boutique, or some activity requiring equipment like a beauty parlor; or relatively low, as in a handicraft or service business that can be operated from home, with materials and advertising the biggest items in the budget. In either case, if a start can be made without recourse to borrowing, fine; if you must borrow, borrow from a bank, not from relatives or friends.

Open a bank account for your proprietorship or corporation, and *get to know your banker*. Go in and ask intelligent questions, seek advice when you need it, have a few short, pertinent interviews with your banker so you become known and give the impression of a reliable person who knows where she's going. This will be invaluable when you want to help in expanding the business or require a lift over a lean period.

And, in such interviews, always, *always*, tell the truth. Don't magnify your assets, and if things are bad, say so and give your ideas for improving them. Being truthful also pays with suppliers and clients, with everyone. In the long run, it earns priceless respect.

When your business has begun to grow, if you have added employees, don't, Ms. Dratler advises, expect them to be your partners. In other words, *you* may be so interested as to devote every waking hour to your business, but don't demand this of your employees. Above all, avoid the hate-women syndrome that Ms. Dratler has noted among some women bosses. Women, she finds—at least some women—are inclined to be hard on other women.

What about a marriage and career combination? Ms. Dratler, who has been married for some 25 years to Adolph Hendler, graphics expert, has run a house and brought up a daughter while steadily developing her business career. A major in marketing and advertising at the College of the City of New York, she started as a market analyst, switched to writing and became chief copy writer for Charles A. Weeks Advertising Company; was advertising manager for Jiffy Manufacturing Company; then, with Jiffy as her first client, opened her own advertising agency and headed it until 1971, when she entered publishing, getting out *Specialty Foods Magazine* (later *Fine Foods & Beverages International*) and *Gusto International Magazine*. She is now Director of Food Forum, Inc., a marketing and communications organization for maximizing sales of fine foods and beverages and offering such services as product research, sales promotion, and packaging and label design.

ZIRA GREENSPAN KAPLAN
SHE TURNED A $50,000 DEFICIT INTO A
HALF MILLION DOLLAR VOLUME

In the 1930's, when Zira Greenspan was 12, fate

projected her into the male business world before she could make the choice between the traditional female role and the invasion of what was then male territory. At that time, her father, Aaron Schneider, ran a small, depression-buffeted appliance store. He needed help and she needed pocket money and a summer job.

As the years went from depression to war time, things went from bad to worse. New refrigerators were not available, so the main source of income was the repair, rehabilitation, and resale of old refrigerators, accompanied by sulpher dioxide leaks, in a building heated by a pot-bellied stove. When the war ended the scene changed to a cleaner new appliance store and Zira learned how to sell appliances and later to remodel kitchens. She did well at kitchen design and the taste of success was heady.

But suddenly in the 1950's the appliance market was saturated and volume plummeted. The question then became how to turn a failing business, with a debt of $50,000 and climbing rapidly, into a success?

Zira took the responsibility of creating drastic change. The problem was that the competitive pressure created by the huge appliance industry, whose success depended on always greater production, left no room for the profit of the retailer. If he couldn't make it, he was expendable. The lesson Zira learned here was that people are only concerned with your success if there is an advantage to them. At that time (not so much now, she says), the furniture industry was made up of thousands of small manufacturers, struggling just as retailers were. It was to their interest to be helpful and earn loyalty from dealers. Some of these sources gave Zira credit which, she says, she didn't deserve, because their need outweighed their risk. The furniture industry was slower paced than that of appliances; the sales representatives took the time to teach Zira and to recommend suitable managerial and sales help. And so, there was a complete change from a heavily discounted appliance store to a profitable furniture store.

Zira spent the next twenty years pulling that business out of its deficit toward the profitable half million dollar yearly volume it finally attained. The profit that was not plowed back into the business was used to rebuild that tired old family-owned building which, as it became more attractive, helped increase the furniture sales.

The final outcome was that a larger furniture merchant wanted this very attractive building as a branch store. Zira gave him the lease. Thus, the building she spent her profit on became profitable.

The lesson she learned was that success takes a lot of hard work, a willingness to keep on learning, and the ability to take risks. Because life is about taking risks.

About being a woman in a man's world, she was always very careful not to allow herself tantrums, unreasonable or illogical behavior that might be attributed to her femininity. She has had employees tell her of their apprehension about taking a job under a woman boss, apprehension which was later resolved. If a man offered her an inside price or was otherwise helpful because he liked her smile or felt chivalrous, she enjoyed the advantage. She feels that part of success is to be shrewd enough to use all the advantages, short of dishonesty.

Today, Zira is retired, a youthful, dynamic blonde, with two grown daughters from her first marriage, and remarried to a Vice President of a major bank. She is active in SCORE (Service Corps of Retired Executives), a volunteer adjunct to the Small Business Administration, which advises people with business problems.

She is not at all sure that she won't invade that man's world again when another challenging situation presents itself, possibly in the area of designing and building homes. Having designed and contracted the construction of her own home in 1960, a house which has been pronounced outstanding, she feels she has a talent in that direction. She says, "Watch out, men. Your world is too interesting to allow it to pass me by."

BONNIE CASHIN
SHE'S TOPS IN FASHION

"Be aware of the world around you." Bonnie Cashin lives by this philosophy and has translated it into the terms of her life and work. Her specialty is today's woman—how she looks and what she does—and Bonnie expresses these findings in the outstanding clothes she designs. Winner of numerous fashion awards at home and abroad, she blends glamour with easy and natural wearing qualities in her garments. When she was chosen for the Fashion Critics Hall of Fame Award in 1972, it was said of her, "Bonnie is closer kin to the first desert wanderer to draw on a djellaba, or the first Indian to cut hide into clothing, than she is what's generally called a fashion designer. The Nomad and the Indian were thinking first about climate, comfort, and practicality; so, always, is she. It would be accurate to describe Bonnie's clothes as always contemporary, even more accurate to leave the adjectives alone and just call them Cashins. They are uniquely her own." A visit to her studio in UN Plaza on New York's East River shows them also to be flowing in line and aglow with color.

Has Bonnie Cashin advice for other women in business? Not especially for women. She believes everyone, man or woman, should follow his own drum beat. Find yourself, be yourself, develop yourself into an outgoing person who has something to give and knows it. Then doors will open and what the individual has to contribute will be honest and of value, because of talent, work, and sincerity. Make it on your own, not because you are a woman—or a man—but a person.

For that matter, what is this "making it"? Gertrude Stein said of the expression "getting there" that people who reached for "there" usually found it wasn't there. So, counsels Bonnie Cashin, dispense with ephemeral "its" and "theres." Reality is being true to oneself.

Bonnie herself found her field early. Her first toys were fabrics. Her mother had a custom dressmaking shop in San Francisco and Los Angeles. Besides learning all about fine sewing in her childhood, Bonnie inherited a talent for painting from her father, an artist, photographer, and inventor. Heredity and environment favored the career she followed, that of creation and design.

A first experience working with a sportswear house on New York's Seventh Avenue led to a motion picture contract, which in turn brought her 60 screen credits. Also, in the beginning days, she designed for dancers (and has continued always to be interested in the dance). When she won two top fashion awards, she decided to gamble and establish Bonnie Cashin Designs.

As an independent, Bonnie Cashin has strong and directional influence on the world's sportswear, knitwear, rainwear, and leather industries. There is a Bonnie Cashin shop in Liberty's of London, and in the late '60's a graphics show of her works was held in London, the first for an American designer.

"Creativity is not a group activity," she says, "it's a lonely business. Getting away when necessary is an artist's right." However, she is no recluse. Her New York apartment is a hospitable one and she makes friends not only in the fashion world but with people in many walks of life. She travels a great deal, and not only to fashion market places. Friends of many cultural and ethnic groups enrich her life.

Education, to Bonnie Cashin, is a continuing process, one in which she both gives and receives. Several years ago, for instance, she was invited by the government of India and the Ford Foundation to participate in planning the revitalization of their handloom industry.

One of her most cherished tributes came when she

received the Philadelphia Museum College of Arts Citation: "Bonnie Cashin is a one-woman United Nations."

SUSAN EDMONDSON
HER BUSINESS SNOWBALLED INTO EIGHT FIGURES!

Her first mail order catalogue in 1974 went out to a list of 30,000 and got a response of 2-2½%. Her current catalogue went out to two and a half million people. She is looking to top $10,000,000 in gross sales.

Who is she? She is Susan Edmondson of Atlanta, Ga., President of Kaleidoscope, Inc.

Susan began her business life as a school teacher. Then she was a counselor for adolescents. A long way from a mail order business. She might never have gone into the new line of work if her husband, Charles, had not been associated with a printing concern. Through this connection she met people who were in mail order companies, became interested in their problems and solutions, and the next step was going around the country visiting and observing these firms.

When she decided to go into the business, she first incorporated, no doubt to show everyone, including herself, that she was in earnest, and then took off for the first trade show in Atlantic City. The show featured china, glass, and other gift merchandise and she decided her first catalogue would be on such items, for gifts and for keeping.

The manufacturers exhibiting at the show must have scented a success in the offing because Susan received an especially cordial reception and plenty of useful tips.

She returned home with her samples of merchandise and was faced with getting out catalogue No. 1. Incidentally, she was operating from a converted carriage house back of her home.

The first catalogue was 16 pages, black and white, 8½" x 5" in size. Susan's partner, with his printing background, helped her write the copy and design and lay out the pages.

The catalogue's mailing was preceded by small ads in *House & Garden* and *House Beautiful* in the spring, then in July they mailed the 30,000 copies. The response was encouraging enough to keep Susan happy in her new project. There were a few disappointments in the original batch of items, one so overstocked that she is still trying to make it move, but, on the whole, her choices proved popular.

Subsequent business has snowballed. The Kaleidoscope catalogues now are all color, with 8½" x 11" pages, handsome jobs, all of them, covering some 300 items.

Susan still edits the copy. She also selects the items—every one of them, she says—gets them in and on the shelves of the warehouse. In addition, she is totally responsible for the production of the catalogues.

Since November, 1975, her partner has joined her full time and he handles purchasing, order processing, customer service, data processing, accounting, and shipping. Kaleidoscope employs about 125 helpers, and honors credit cards—Master Charge, American Express, Diners Club, and Bank-Americard. They have installed a toll-free number and now attribute some 20% of their sales dollars to this telephone service. There are six incoming WATS, manned from 8:30 a.m. until 11:00 p.m., seven days a week. Real voices answer until 11 o'clock, when a recording device goes on, but, even then, Susan, if she is around, sometimes answers herself. Kaleidoscope is all for personal contact.

Kaleidoscope now offers jewelry, fashion designer ready-to-wear, gifts, furniture and decorative accessories, and original, limited edition art.

The chief headache in this kind of business, says Susan, is the chance you must take in selecting an article. Sometimes it doesn't appeal, or sometimes when it does you have ordered too many. Susan and her partner are solving the problem of overstocked merchandise by opening a retail store in Atlanta.

Asked in a recent interview to what she owes her firm's phenomenal success, Susan hesitated, then said finally, "I don't know!"

However, the observer can make an educated guess.

Susan considers her business a specialty shop by mail, with items that the customer might not be able to find in local stores. She chooses her merchandise by asking herself whether she would like to own that particular item or give it as a gift to a relative or friend. Many Kaleidoscope items are exclusives. Susan tries to specify that they be exclusive, at least for the life of the catalogue. Many items are imported. Kaleidoscope gets out orders promptly.

It all adds up. In Susan Edmondson's case, to eight figures.

APPENDIX

Below is listed information sources to help you in selecting, starting, and implementing your business. These sources encompass a wide range of information, including: financing, marketing, management, advertising and promotion, direct mail, record keeping, assessing profitability. They can serve you as a continuing at-your-fingertips reference to provide answers to basic questions.

BANK OF AMERICA

The Bank of America's *Small Business Reporter* is for everyone needing small business information. *Business Operations* describe and explain various aspects of business management and operation. *Business Profiles* deal with specific businesses, investment requirements, operational format of each, and opportunities. These pamphlets are obtainable at most branches, or by writing to Bank of America, P.O. Box 37,000, San Francisco, California 94137. The cost of the pamphlets is $1.00 each.

BUSINESS OPERATIONS:

Vol./No.		TITLE
7	7	Opening Your Own Business: A Personal Appraisal
7	11	Understanding Financial Statements
8	5	Financing Small Business
8	11	How To Buy or Sell a Business
9	1	Advertising
9	8	Personnel for Small Business
9	9	Franchising
10	4	Retail Financial Records
10	5	Marketing New Product Ideas
10	10	Steps To Starting a Business
10	12	Management Succession
11	3	Business Management: Advice from Consultants
11	5	Avoiding Management Pitfalls
12	6	Exporting
13	1	Crime Prevention for Small Businesses
		Special Issue Beating the Cash Crisis

BUSINESS PROFILES:

Vol./No.		TITLE
9	5	Small Job Printing
9	12	Drug Stores
10	3	Apparel Manufacturing
10	6	Equipment Rental Business
10	8	The Handcraft Business
10	9	Repair Services
10	11	Sporting Goods Stores
11	1	Home Furnishings Stores
11	2	Health Food Stores
11	4	Liquor Stores
11	6	Bookstores
11	7	Mail Order Enterprises
11	8	Day Care
11	9	Bars and Cocktail Lounges
11	10	Sewing and Needlecraft Centers
12	1	Bicycle Stores
12	2	Apparel Stores
12	3	Building Maintenance Services
12	4	Plant Shops
12	5	Shoe Stores
12	7	Camera Shops
12	8	Restaurants and Food Services
12	9	Hairgrooming/Beauty Salons
12	10	Toy and Hobby/Craft Stores
13	2	Dry Cleaning Services
13	3	Consumer Electronics Centers
13	4	Gift Stores
13	5	Auto Supply Stores

CHAMBERS OF COMMERCE

Your Chamber of Commerce serves as a clearing house for all activity which will develop a better business climate and a better city for each business concern and its employees. Chambers of Commerce are valuable for consultation as to the need for a business like yours in the community, the competition to be faced, and desirable location.

CONSUMERS REGISTER OF AMERICAN BUSINESS

17,000 corporations that manufacture or market 95% of all U.S. consumer products and services (contains complete address and telephone numbers). $72.50. National Register Publishing Company, 5201 Old Orchard Road, Skokie, Illinois 60076.

COUNCIL OF BETTER BUSINESS BUREAUS

Better Business Bureaus affiliated offices are located throughout the country, in virtually every metropolitan area. The New York chapter is located at 110 Fifth Avenue. BBB constitutes a "goldmine" of information on business—particularly fraudulent practices, and how to avoid them. They also maintain records of companies whose past practices have been dubious. They publish books on business—also a pamphlet on franchising which can constitute helpful information for the person seeking to enter a business.

DUN & BRADSTREET

This company publishes financial reports, business ratios, and varied business advisory booklets—all highly helpful and supportive to the business person seeking to enter and succeed in business. Departments on Credit Report Service, Business Economics, Sales Marketing, Exporters Encyclopedia, International Marketing Guides, World Marketing, etc., are located at 99 Church Street, New York, New York. A spacious library is also located there. Dun & Bradstreet Publications Corporation, inclusive of Education Center, Executive Readers' Service, and Systems and Seminars Department are located at 666 Fifth Avenue, New York, New York.

EXPORT

Trade Channel, a publication issued monthly, rotated to

over 200,000 selected firms; Edition 1 covers Europe, U.S.A.
and Canada, Australia, Oceania, and New Zealand; Edition 2
covers Africa, Asia, Central and South America, and the
Caribbean. Eugene Smith, Director, Suite 86013, 1 World
Trade Center, New York, New York 10048. Each edition:
$12.00 a year.

FRANCHISING INFORMATION

Booklets and other informational data on franchising
include: Franchise Opportunities Handbook, U.S. Department of Commerce. For sale by: Superintendent of Documents, U.S. Government Printing Office, Washington, D.C.
20402. Price: $3.10.

Directory of Franchising Organizations: Revised annually. Pilot Industries, Inc., 347 Fifth Avenue, New York, New
York 10016. Price: $2.50. A comprehensive listing of the
nation's top money-making franchises with concise description and approximate investment. Includes important facts
about franchising and evaluation check list.

Franchising: Small Business Reporter, Bank of America
Marketing Publication, Post Office Box 37000, San Francisco,
California 94137. Volume 9, Number 9. 1970. pp 1-12. Price:
$1.00. This report examines various franchise systems, the
franchisor/franchisee relationship, the franchise agreement,
finding and evaluating a franchise, franchising and its critics,
legislation and arbitration, etc. Sources of further information
are noted.

*Franchising: Its Nature Scope, Advantages and Develop-
ment:* Charles L. Vaughn, D.D. Heath and Company, 125
Spring Street, Lexington, Massachusetts 02173. 1974. 208 pp.
Price: $12.00. A comprehensive overview of the nature, scope,
and history of franchising as well as practical advice and
information to students of marketing, potential franchisors
and franchisees, and large companies contemplating entering

the field. Notes, tables, figures, index, bibliography, appendixes.

LIBRARIES

The public libraries offer information, basic and supplementary, on almost any subject, from accounting to zoology. If your public library does not have a book you need, the librarian can probably borrow it for you from another library for a specified time. Also, there are college and university libraries, where you can consult theses and treatises on subjects relating to your business.

UNITED STATES GOVERNMENT

The United States Government has a vast number of agencies, programs, and activities to help businesses. Answers to many vital questions are provided.

ALABAMA
Birmingham: 322-8591. Toll-free tieline to Atlanta, Ga.
Mobile: 438-1421. Toll-free tieline to New Orleans, La.

ARIZONA
Phoenix: (602) 261-3313. Federal Bldg., 230 N. 1st Avenue 85025
Tucson: 622-1511. Toll-free tieline to Phoenix, Ariz.

ARKANSAS
Little Rock. 378-6177. Toll-free tieline to Memphis, Tenn.

CALIFORNIA
Los Angeles: (213) 688-3800. Federal Bldg., 300 N. Los Angeles
    Street 90012
Sacramento: (916) 449-3344. Federal Bldg.—U.S. Courthouse,
    650 Capitol Mall 95814
San Diego: (714) 293-6030. 202 C Street 92101
San Francisco: (415) 556-6600. Federal Bldg.—U.S. Courthouse,
    450 Golden Gate Avenue 94102
San Jose: 275-7422. Toll-free tieline to San Francisco, Calif.

COLORADO
Colorado Springs: 471-9491. Toll-free tieline to Denver, Colo.
Denver: (303) 837-3602. Federal Bldg., 1961 Stout Street 80202
Pueblo: 544-9523. Toll-free tieline to Denver, Colo.

CONNECTICUT
Hartford: 527-2617. Toll-free tieline to New York, N.Y.
New Haven: 624-4720. Toll-free tieline to New York, N.Y.

DISTRICT OF COLUMBIA
Washington: (202) 755-8660. 7th & D Streets, S.W., Rm. 5716
    20407

FLORIDA
Fort Lauderdale: 522-8531. Toll-free tieline to Miami, Fla.
Jacksonville: 354-4756. Toll-free tieline to St. Petersburg, Fla.
Miami: (305) 350-4155. Federal Bldg., 51 Southwest 1st Avenue
    33130
St. Petersburg: (813) 893-3495. William C. Cramer, Federal Bldg.,
    144 1st Avenue, S. 33701
Tampa: 229-7911. Toll-free tieline to St. Petersburg, Fla.
West Palm Beach: 833-7566. Toll-free tieline to Miami, Fla.

GEORGIA
Atlanta: (404) 526-6891. Federal Bldg., 275 Peachtree St., N.E.
    30303

HAWAII
Honolulu: (808) 546-8620. U.S. Post Office, Courthouse &
    Customhouse, 335 Merchant Street 96813

ILLINOIS
Chicago: (312) 353-4242. Everett McKinley Dirksen Bldg., 219 S.
    Dearborn Street 60604

INDIANA
Indianapolis: (317) 269-7373. Federal Bldg., 575 N. Pennsylvania
    46204

IOWA
Des Moines: 282-9091. Toll-free tieline to Omaha, Neb.

KANSAS
Topeka: 232-7229. Toll-free tieline to Kansas City, Mo.
Wichita: 262-6931. Toll-free tieline to Kansas City, Mo.

KENTUCKY
Louisville: (502) 582-6261. Federal Bldg., 600 Federal Place 40202

LOUISIANA
New Orleans: (504) 589-6696. Federal Bldg., Rm. 1210, 701
    Loyola Avenue 70113

MARYLAND
Baltimore: (301) 962-4980. Federal Bldg., 31 Hopkins Plaza 21201

MASSACHUSETTS
Boston: (617) 223-7121. J.F.K. Federal Bldg., Cambridge Street,
Lobby, 1st Floor 02203

MICHIGAN
Detroit: (313) 226-7016. Federal Bldg., U.S. Courthouse, 231 W.
Lafayette Street 48226

MINNESOTA
Minneapolis: (612) 725-2073. Federal Bldg., U.S. Courthouse, 110
S. 4th Street 55401

MISSOURI
Kansas City: (816) 374-2466. Federal Bldg., 601 E. 12th St. 64106
St. Joseph: 233-8206. Toll-free tieline to Kansas City, Mo.
St. Louis: (314) 425-4106. Federal Bldg., 1520 Market Street 63103

NEBRASKA
Omaha: (402) 221-3353. Federal Bldg., U.S. Post Office & Courthouse, 215 N. 17th Street 68102

NEW JERSEY
Newark: (201) 645-3600. Federal Bldg., 970 Broad Street 07102
Trenton: 396-4400. Toll-free tieline to Newark, N.J.

NEW MEXICO
Albuquerque: (505) 766-3091. Federal Bldg., U.S. Courthouse,
500 Gold Avenue, S.W. 87101
Santa Fe: 983-7743. Toll-free tieline to Albuquerque, N.M.

NEW YORK
Albany: 463-4421. Toll-free tieline to New York, N.Y.
Buffalo: (716) 842-5770. Federal Bldg., 111 W. Huron St. 14202
New York: (212) 264-4464. Lobby, Federal Bldg., 26 Federal
Plaza 10007
Rochester: 546-5075. Toll-free tieline to Buffalo, N.Y.
Syracuse: 476-8545. Toll-free tieline to Buffalo, N.Y.

NORTH CAROLINA
Charlotte: 376-3600. Toll-free tieline to Atlanta, Ga.

OHIO
Akron: 375-5475. Toll-free tieline to Cleveland, Ohio
Cincinnati: (513) 684-2801. Federal Bldg., 550 Main Street 45202
Cleveland: (216) 522-4040. Federal Bldg., 1240 E. 9th Street 44199
Columbus: 221-1014. Toll-free tieline to Cincinnati, Ohio
Dayton: 223-7377. Toll-free tieline to Cincinnati, Ohio
Toledo: 244-8625. Toll-free tieline to Cleveland, Ohio

OKLAHOMA
Oklahoma City: (405) 231-4868. U.S. Post Office & Courthouse,
    201 N.W. 3rd Street 73102
Tulsa: 584-4193. Toll-free tieline to Oklahoma City, Okla.

OREGON
Portland: (503) 221-2222. Federal Bldg., 1220 S.W. 3rd Avenue
    97204

PENNSYLVANIA
Philadelphia: (215) 597-7042. Federal Bldg., 600 Arch Street 19106
Pittsburgh: (412) 644-3456. Federal Bldg., 1000 Liberty Ave. 15222
Scranton: 346-7081. Toll-free tieline to Philadelphia, Pa.

RHODE ISLAND
Providence: 331-5565. Toll-free tieline to Boston, Mass.

TENNESSEE
Chattanooga: 265-8231. Toll-free tieline to Memphis, Tenn.
Memphis: (901) 534-3285. Clifford Davis Federal Bldg., 167 N.
    Main Street 38103

TEXAS
Austin: 472-5494. Toll-free tieline to Houston, Texas
Dallas: 749-2131. Toll-free tieline to Fort Worth, Texas
Fort Worth: (817) 334-3624. Fritz Garland Lanham Federal Bldg.,
    819 Taylor Street 76102
Houston: (713) 226-5711. Federal Bldg., U.S. Courthouse, 515
    Rusk Avenue 77002
San Antonio: 224-4471. Toll-free tieline to Houston, Texas

UTAH
Ogden: 399-1347. Toll-free tieline to Salt Lake City, Utah
Salt Lake City: (801) 524-5353. Federal Bldg., U.S. Post Office,
    Courthouse, 124 S. State Street 84138

WASHINGTON
Seattle: (206) 442-0570. Federal Bldg., 915 2nd Avenue 98174
Tacoma: 383-5230. Toll-free tieline to Seattle, Wash.

WISCONSIN
Milwaukee: 271-2273. Toll-free tieline to Chicago, Ill.

The Federal Information Centers are a joint venture of
the U.S. General Services Administration and the U.S. Civil
Service Commission.

In the local calling area of the cities served by tie-lines, the number listed will connect you with the nearest FIC at no charge.

INTERNAL REVENUE SERVICE

The IRS offers a number of services designed to assist new business people in understanding and meeting their Federal tax obligations. *Mr. Businessman's Kit* (publication #454), containing informative publications, forms, instructions, and samples of notices which the IRS issues to business concerns, is available free. Also free is *The Tax Guide for Small Business* (publication #334), which can be obtained at local IRS offices and from the District Director, or the Superintendent of Documents, U.S. Government Printing Office, Washington, D.C. 20403.

OFFICE OF MINORITY BUSINESS ENTERPRISES

OMBE was established within the Department of Commerce to be the focal point of the Federal Government's efforts to assist the establishment of new minority enterprises and the expansion of existing ones. Women are not a minority, but, since they have some of the problems of a minority, OMBE can be approached from this aspect. Besides the Regional Offices listed below, OMBE operates 13 field offices and has affiliated with private non-profit business development organizations. OMBE assists in funding administrative costs of these centers which serve as a central information source on business opportunities and provide management and technical assistance to individual business people. Addresses of Field Offices and Funding Organizations can be obtained from the Regional Offices:

1372 Peachtree St., N.E.
Suite 505
Atlanta, Ga. 30309

26 Federal Plaza
Room 1307
New York, N.Y. 10007

55 E. Monroe St.	15043 Federal Bldg.
Suite 1438	450 Golden Gate Ave.
Chicago, Ill. 60603	San Francisco, Ca. 94102
1412 Main St.	1730 K St., N.W.
Suite 1702	Suite 420
Dallas, Texas 75202	Washington, D.C. 20006

SMALL BUSINESS ADMINISTRATION

This organization renders assistance in various ways to those planning to enter business as well as to those in business. This assistance includes counseling and possible financial aid. Counseling may be by SBA specialists or retired executives under the Service Corps of Retired Executives (SCORE) program, and could include seminars or courses, or a combination of services including reference publications.

FREE MANAGEMENT ASSISTANCE PUBLICATIONS

MANAGEMENT AIDS

These leaflets deal with functional problems in small manufacturing plants and concentrate on subjects of interest to administrative executives.

...... 32. How Trade Associations Help Small Business
...... 46. How To Analyze Your Own Business
...... 49. Know Your Patenting Procedures
...... 80. Choosing the Legal Structure for Your Firm
...... 82. Reducing the Risks in Product Development
...... 85. Analyzing Your Cost of Marketing
...... 92. Wishing Won't Get Profitable New Products
......111. Steps in Incorporating a Business
......161. Proving Fidelity Losses
......162. Keeping Machines and Operators Productive
......169. Designing Small Plans for Economy and Flexibility
......170. The ABC's of Borrowing
......174. Is Your Cash Supply Adequate?
......176. Financial Audits: A Tool for Better Management
......177. Planning and Controlling Production for Efficiency
......178. Effective Industrial Advertising for Small Plants
......179. Breaking the Barriers to Small Business Planning

TECHNICAL AIDS

These leaflets are intended for top technical personnel in small concerns or for technical specialists who supervise that part of the company's operations.

...... 86. PERT/CPM Management System for the Small Sub-
           contractor
...... 87. Value Analysis for Small Business
...... 90. Welding and Flame-Cutting Processes and Practices
...... 91. A Tested System for Achieving Quality Control
...... 92. Using Adhesives in Small Plants

SMALL MARKETERS' AIDS

These leaflets provide suggestions and management guidelines for small retail, wholesale, and service firms.

...... 25. Are You Kidding Yourself About Your Profits?
...... 71. Checklist for Going Into Business
...... 95. Are Your Salespeople Missing Opportunities?
...... 96. Checklist for Successful Retail Advertising
......104. Preventing Accidents in Small Stores
......105. A Pricing Checklist for Managers
......107. Building Strong Relations With Your Bank
......108. Building Repeat Retail Business
......109. Stimulating Impulse Buying for Increased Sales
......110. Controlling Cash in Small Retail and Service Firms
......111. Interior Display: A Way To Increase Sales
......113. Quality and Taste as Sales Appeals
......114. Pleasing Your Boss, The Customer
......115. Are You Ready for Franchising?
......116. How To Select a Resident Buying Office
......118. Legal Services for Small Retail and Service Firms
......119. Preventing Retail Theft
......121. Measuring the Results of Advertising
......122. Controlling Inventory in Small Wholesale Firms
......123. Stock Control for Small Stores
......124. Knowing Your Image
......125. Pointers on Display Lighting
......126. Accounting Services for Small Service Firms
......127. Six Methods for Success in a Small Store
......128. Building Customer Confidence in Your Service Shop
......129. Reducing Shoplifting Losses
......130. Analyze Your Records to Reduce Costs
......132. The Federal Wage-Hour Law in Small Firms
......133. Can You Afford Delivery Service?
......134. Preventing Burglary and Robbery Loss
......135. Arbitration: Peace-Maker in Small Business
......136. Hiring the Right Man
......137. Outwitting Bad Check Passers
......138. Sweeping Profit Out the Back Door
......139. Understanding Truth-in-Lending
......140. Profit By Your Wholesalers' Services
......141. Danger Signals in a Small Store

SMALL BUSINESS BIBLIOGRAPHIES
(No mailing list for this series.)

These leaflets furnish reference sources for individual types of businesses.

...... 55. Wholesaling
...... 56. Training Commercial Salesmen
...... 58. Automation for Small Offices
...... 60. Painting and Wall Decorating
...... 64. Photographic Dealers and Studios
...... 66. Motels
...... 67. Manufacturers' Sales Representative
...... 69. Machine Shop—Job Type
...... 72. Personnel Management
...... 75. Inventory Management

SBA FIELD OFFICE ADDRESSES

Boston	Mass. 02114, 150 Causeway St.
Holyoke	Mass. 01040, 326 Appleton St.
Augusta	Maine 04330, Federal Bldg., U.S. Post Office, 40 Western Ave.
Concord	New Hampshire 03301, 55 Pleasant St.
Hartford	Conn. 06103, Fed. Office Bldg., 450 Maine St.
Montpelier	Vt. 05602, Fed. Bldg., 2nd Fl., 87 State St.
Providence	R.I. 02903, 702 Smith Bldg., 57 Eddy St.
New York	N.Y. 10007, 26 Federal Plaza, Rm. 3100
Hato Rey	P.R. 00919, 255 Ponce De Leon Ave.
Newark	N.J. 07102, 970 Broad St., Rm. 1635
Syracuse	N.Y. 13202, Hunter Plaza, Fayette/Salina Sts.
Buffalo	N.Y. 14202, 111 W. Huron St.
Albany	N.Y. 12207, 99 Washington Ave.
Rochester	N.Y. 14604, 55 St. Paul St.
Philadelphia	Bala Cynwyd, Pa. 19004, One Bala Cynwood Plaza
Harrisburg	Pa. 17108, 1500 N. Second St.
Wilkes-Barre	Pa. 18703, 34 S. Main St.
Baltimore	Towson, Md. 21204, 7800 York Rd.
Wilmington	Del. 19801, 844 King St.
Clarksburg	W. Va. 26301, Lowndes Bank Bldg., 109 N. Third St.
Charleston	W. Va. 25301, Charleston Natl. Plaza, Ste. 628
Pittsburgh	Pa. 15222, Fed. Bldg., 1000 Liberty Ave.
Richmond	Va. 23240, Fed. Bldg., 400 N. Eighth St.
Washington	D.C. 20417, 1030 15th St., N.W., Rm. 250
Atlanta	Ga. 30309, 1401 Peachtree St., N.E.
Biloxi	Miss. 39530, 111 Fred Haise Bldg.
Birmingham	Ala. 35205, 908 S. 20th St.
Charlotte	N.C. 28202, Addison Bldg., 222 S. Church St.
Columbia	S.C. 29201, 1801 Assembly St.
Coral Gables	Fla. 33134, 2222 Ponce de Leon Blvd.

Jackson	Miss. 39205, Petroleum Bldg., Pascagoula and Amite Sts.
Jacksonville	Fla. 32202, Fed. Office Bldg., 400 W. Bay St.
Louisville	Ky. 40202, Fed. Office Bldg., 600 Federal Pl.
Tampa	Fla. 33607, Fed. Bldg., 500 Zack St.
Nashville	Tenn. 37219, 404 James Robertson Pkwy.
Knoxville	Tenn. 37902, 502 S. Gay St.
Memphis	Tenn. 38103, Fed. Bldg., 167 N. Main St.
Chicago	Ill. 60604, Fed. Off. Bldg., 219 S. Dearborn St.
Springfield	Ill. 62701, 502 E. Monroe St.
Cleveland	Ohio 44199, 1240 E. 9th St.
Columbus	Ohio 43215, 34 N. High St.
Cincinnati	Ohio 45202, Fed. Bldg., 550 Main St.
Detroit	Mich. 48226, 1249 Washington Blvd.
Marquette	Mich. 49855, 201 McClellan St.
Indianapolis	Ind. 46204, 575 N. Pennsylvania St.
Madison	Wis. 53703, 122 W. Washington Ave.
Milwaukee	Wis. 53203, 735 W. Wisconsin Ave.
Eau Claire	Wis. 54701, 500 S. Barstow St.
Minneapolis	Minn. 55402, 12 S. Sixth St.

Dallas	Texas 75202, 1100 Commerce St.
Albuquerque	N.M. 87110, 5000 Marble Ave., N.E.
Houston	Texas 77002, 808 Travis St.
Little Rock	Ark. 72201, 611 Gaines St.
Lubbock	Texas 79408, 1205 Texas Ave.
El Paso	Texas 79901, 109 N. Oregon St.
Lower Rio Grande Valley	Harlingen, Texas 78550, 219 E. Jackson St.
Corpus Christi	Texas 78408, 3105 Leopard St.
Marshall	Texas 75670, 505 E. Travis St.
New Orleans	La. 70113, 1001 Howard Ave.
Oklahoma City	Okla. 73118, 50 Penn Pl.
San Antonio	Texas 78205, 301 Broadway
Kansas City	Mo. 64106, 911 Walnut St.
Des Moines	Iowa 50309, New Fed. Bldg., 210 Walnut St.
Omaha	Neb. 68102, Fed. Bldg., 215 N. 17th St.
St. Louis	Mo. 63101, Fed. Bldg., 210 N. 12th St.
Wichita	Kan. 67202, 120 S. Market St.

Denver	Colo. 80202, 721 19th St., Rm. 426
Casper	Wyo. 82601, 100 East B St.
Fargo	N.D. 58102, 653 2nd Ave., N.
Helena	Mont. 59601, 613 Helena Ave.
Salt Lake City	Utah 84138, Fed. Bldg., 125 S. State St.
Sioux Falls	S.D. 57102, Natl. Bank Bldg., 8th & Main Ave.

San Francisco	Calif. 94102, Fed. Bldg., 450 Golden Gate Ave.
Fresno	Calif. 93721, Fed. Bldg., 1130 O Street

Honolulu	Hawaii 96813, 1149 Bethel St.
Agana	Guam 96910, Ada Plaza Center Bldg.
Los Angeles	Calif. 90014, 849 S. Broadway
Las Vegas	Nev. 89121, 301 E. Stewart
Phoenix	Ariz. 85004, 112 N. Central Ave.
San Diego	Calif. 92101, 110 West C St.
Seattle	Wash. 98104, 710 Second Ave.
Anchorage	Alaska 99501, 1016 W. Sixth Ave.
Fairbanks	Alaska 99701, 501½ Second Ave.
Boise	Idaho 83701, 216 N. Eighth St.
Portland	Ore. 97205, 921 Southwest Washington St.
Spokane	Wash. 99210, Courthouse Bldg., Rm. 651

WRITING

Two professional publications:

THE WRITER
8 Arlington St.
Boston, Mass. 02116

WRITERS DIGEST
9933 Alliance Rd.
Cincinnati, Ohio 45232